"My experiences with Apple and Canva have taught me that an ecosystem is a beautiful thing. This book will help you build your ecosystem in a beautiful way. If you have a great product, you need Pam's expertise to build your audience."

—**Guy Kawasaki,** chief evangelist at Canva, host of *Remarkable People Podcast*
https://guykawasaki.com/

"Pam Slim is every entrepreneur's dream—a wise and compassionate advisor who will help you grow your enterprise while staying true to your values. *The Widest Net* is a powerful guide to finding new opportunities for your business and new possibilities in yourself."

—**Daniel H. Pink,** author of *When, Drive,* and *To Sell Is Human*
https://www.danpink.com/

"Know your customer," says every business book everywhere. Yeah but . . . how, exactly? Pam's terrific new book unlocks the mystery."

—**Ann Handley,** *Wall Street Journal* bestselling author of two books and chief content officer at MarketingProfs
https://annhandley.com/

"If there's one thing we know, it's that community is the currency of the digital age. And, no one knows more about how to build, nurture, and gather value from communities than Pam Slim. This makes *The Widest Net* hands down the best bang for your buck. Get it, read it, and thank me later on Twitter!"

—Shama Hyder, CEO of Zen Media
https://shamahyder.com/about/

"If you have a product, service, or idea you want to share with the world, you need this book. Pamela Slim shows you how to build a lasting audience in ways that are congruent with your values. This is the guide you need to build a successful business with joy and integrity."

—Dorie Clark, author of *Entrepreneurial You* and executive education faculty, Duke University Fuqua School of Business
https://dorieclark.com/

"As a pattern-finder, I spent my career codifying patterns found in story so others can communicate their best. Pamela Slim's *The Widest Net* does the same for building a large, enthusiastic audience for your product, company or movement."

—Nancy Duarte, best-selling author and CEO of Duarte, Inc.
https://www.duarte.com/

"I have been lucky enough to spend a magical afternoon with Pam in front of her floor-to-ceiling white board shaping our mission for the Non-Obvious Company. For anyone trying to go beyond short-term success and build a large and passionate audience, this book is a time-tested field guide from a generous and kind expert who has done it many times before."

—**Rohit Bhargava,** #1 WSJ bestselling author and founder of the Non-Obvious Company
https://www.nonobvious.com/

"FINALLY! A powerful yet achievable system for turning your ideas into profitable opportunities. An indispensable guide for every start-up entrepreneur and small business owner."

—**Jay Baer,** coauthor of *Talk Triggers: The Complete Guide to Creating Customers with Word of Mouth*
https://www.jaybaer.com/

"*The Widest Net* is the book your business has been begging for! Pam does a great job of tying together the underlying core of your business with the consistent functions that you need to incorporate to make more money. Full of case studies and examples, this book gives you the blueprint to follow on your path to business success. This book will make you a better business owner."

—**Lamar Tyler,** cofounder, Black and Married with Children and Traffic Sales and Profit
https://trafficsalesandprofit.com/

"I have been a fan of Pam's work for close to two decades and she never ceases to amaze me with a unique combination of "fresh thinking," "practicality," and "pursuit of excellence." *The Widest Net* is rich with insights very relevant to current times. Miss reading this and you will regret it."

> **—Rajesh Setty,** cofounder of Audvisor.com, 18x author and teacher
> https://rajeshsetty.com/

"If you want to build a large and passionate community while maintaining your voice, creativity, and integrity, then you must read *The Widest Net*. Its easy-to-follow method will help you explode your business while respecting your values."

> **—Chase Jarvis,** bestselling author of *Creative Calling* and founder of CreativeLive
> https://www.chasejarvis.com/

THE
WIDEST
NET

THE
WIDEST
NET

Unlock Untapped Markets and Discover
New Customers Right in Front of You

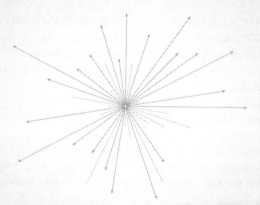

PAMELA SLIM

New York   Chicago   San Francisco   Athens   London   Madrid
Mexico City   Milan   New Delhi   Singapore   Sydney   Toronto

1 2 3 4 5 6 7 8 9   LCR   26 25 24 23 22 21

ISBN   978-1-264-26679-1
MHID   1-264-26679-0

e-ISBN   978-1-264-26680-7
e-MHID 1-264-26680-4

Library of Congress Cataloging-in-Publication Data

Names: Slim, Pamela, author.
Title: The widest net : unlock untapped markets and discover new customers right in front of you / Pamela Slim.
Description: New York : McGraw Hill, [2022] | Includes bibliographical references and index.
Identifiers: LCCN 2021026414 (print) | LCCN 2021026415 (ebook) | ISBN 9781264266791 (hardback) | ISBN 9781264266807 (ebook)
Subjects: LCSH: Relationship marketing. | Customer relations.
Classification: LCC HF5415.55 .S64 2022 (print) | LCC HF5415.55 (ebook) | DDC 658.8/12—dc23
LC record available at https://lccn.loc.gov/2021026414
LC ebook record available at https://lccn.loc.gov/2021026415

McGraw Hill books are available at special quantity discounts to use as premiums and sales promotions or for use in corporate training programs. To contact a representative, please visit the Contact Us pages at www.mhprofessional.com.

To Desirée Adaway, the most natural, skillful, and generous community builder I know. Thank you for teaching me so much over the last four decades. I could not have dreamed up a better best friend. I love you always.

CONTENTS

ACKNOWLEDGMENTS

We love to glorify the idea of a lone writer at the keyboard, braving a field of words with strong coffee and an iron will.

Nothing could be further from the truth for this book. Every idea in *The Widest Net* is informed by a shared experience, either in conversation with individual clients or with groups of people in workshops around the country and in our K'é Main Street Learning Lab. It is through our work together that ideas sprung up, frameworks were created, and inspiration struck.

The physical, mental and spiritual process of writing this book was supported first and foremost by my home crew of Darryl, Joshua, Angie and Naasir (not forgetting our fur babies DC, Rocky and Tsili). You brought me coffee, rubbed my shoulders, left encouraging notes, cracked jokes, and literally kept me going when I felt like I could not continue. I love you and appreciate you deeply.

Jeff and Chawa, watching you build your own beautiful community and physical space at Palabras Bilingual Bookstore and Nurture House was so encouraging and inspiring. Thank you for showing what community healing is about.

The heart of The Widest Net Method was built by the many amazing Key Guardians at K'é Main Street Learning Lab including Isha Cogborn, La'Vista Jones, Ita Udo-Ema, Davina Lyons, Yolanda Facio, Joey Bellus, Eileen Kane, Joe Tafur, Laura Suarez, Belinda Eriacho, Naomi Tsosie, Debbie Nez Manuel, Royce Manuel, Freddie Johnson, Jennifer Gastelum, Tomas Stanton, Cindy Ornstein, Veronica Archer, Angela Garmon, Amanda Blackhorse, Melody Lewis, Turquoise Devereaux, Bobbie Nez, Violet Duncan, Tony Duncan, Bruce Nelson, Stephanie Luz Cordel, Terry Benelli, Ryan Winkle, and Augie Gastelum.

To our thousands of community members and scores of organization partners who attended events over the years, we see you, we love you, and we look forward to continuing our work together.

To the 2015 community tour partners and participants, your insight and feedback was critical to shaping the Widest Net Method. Who knew you would inspire me to open a brick-and-mortar space? I didn't see that coming.

To Mark Otto, my friend and coach, your generosity and willingness to push me to be better has had a profoundly positive impact on my life and business. Thank you!

To my Mastermind buddies Susan Baier and Chris Lee, thank you for five years of excellent advice, shared joy and tears and lots of swearing. We did this!

To my ASU partners Johanna Richards, Jake Pinholster, Nyasha Stone Sheppard, Kristin Slice and JiMi Choi, thank you for bringing me into the exciting new downtown Mesa campus project. It has been a delight working with you.

To Jen Duff and Ivan Martinez, thank you for introducing me to the beauty and possibility of downtown Mesa. Your friendship and inspiration helped bring K'é to life!

To my downtown Mesa neighborhood family including Jarrod and Jace (and extended family!), Luis, Tina, Heather, Orvid, Maria, Rob, Chuck, Kelsey, Jim Bob, Marco, Jenny, Odeen, and all my Main Street businesses, you make neighborhood development joyful.

To my agent Joelle Delbourgo, in the face of rejections, you kept me grounded and found a perfect home for this special book. Thank you for always believing in me!

To David Moldawer, thank you for always being a great friend with a friendly ear and honest voice. Thank you for shaping my proposal and giving me clear and direct feedback when I needed to hear it. I am so lucky I got to work with you. This book literally would not exist without you.

To Donya Dickerson and the entire extended editorial team at McGraw Hill, including Kevin Commins and Steve Strauss, thank you for your care and support of this book. It was so fun to work with a new publishing team. I felt valued, respected, and trusted throughout this entire process.

To the audio book team at Penguin, I am so thankful I get to add the third book to the trilogy!

To Jules Taggart, Omar Morales, Rennel Parino, Caiti Franscell, Johanna Lopez and the entire WayWard Kind team, thank you for your excellent marketing partnership!

To Clay Hebert, thank you for your generosity of spirit and amazing ability to craft book titles and subtitles! You saved me.

To Will Weiser, Nikki Papadopoulos, and Seth Godin, thank you for your long-term conversations about and encouragement for this book. I would not have gotten here without your honest feedback.

To Trena White and the Page Two Team and Rohit Bhargava and the Ideapress Publishing Team, thank you for encouraging me to write this book and demonstrating generous partnership and community building. Your authors are so lucky to work with you!

To Desiree, Ericka, Nicole, Jessica, and Jules, our GIF-filled text chats give me life and inspiration. I love you all dearly. To Michele, thank you for always being willing to coach me off a ledge. I love you. To La'Vista, you make me a better person and professional. Thank you for your excellent partnership in support of our clients! To Hiro, thank you for helping me connect with the deva of my book. To Charlie and Jonathan, thank you for being the best brothers from another mother.

To Karley Cunningham, Violet Duncan, Jeff Goins, Susan Baier, Greg Hartle, Michael Margolis, Wes Kao, Brian Clark, Sean Blanda, Bob Moore, Heather Krause, Desiree Adaway, Debbie Reber, André Blackman, Lamar Tyler, Daryl Garcia, Hajj Flemings, Brian Shea, Joel Louis, Kyle Durand, Guy Kawasaki, Caleb Gardner, and Christopher Penn, thank you for being generous, open and vulnerable enough to share your experience and insight with *The Widest Net* readers. To Skip Miller, thank you for teaching me to not be afraid of selling.

Finally, to my clients. It is my greatest joy and honor to help you bring your world-changing work to life. Thank you for your courage, tenacity, and, most importantly, laughter. I love you all.

INTRODUCTION

Just because someone stumbles and loses
their path, doesn't mean they're lost forever.
—**Charles Xavier,** *X-Men*

Karley Cunningham was the embodiment of a successful entrepreneur.

She was an expert in her field of business branding. She had fierce discipline in her creative process and centered her clients in her business model. No one cared more about client outcomes than Karley. She had a track record of client success.

As for grit, tenacity, and discipline, she was filled with it, starting at the tender age of six as an elite figure skater in her home country of Canada. In her twenties, she raced as a pro elite mountain biker with the Canadian women's team. Karley ran toward challenges, the tougher the better.

Her branding firm had been cruising along and growing at a healthy rate for three years, driven by her robust referral network. Work was so busy that she brought her wife Elise into the business full-time, to work on systems and client project management.

Karley's closing rate once she got a qualified prospect on the phone was about 80 percent. Things were great. Until one day they weren't.

Karley said: "Our revenue stream slowly started to decrease. The phone stopped ringing, and when you put a new prospect in front of me, all of a sudden, I couldn't close a deal to save my life. All the growth we had seen went backward. Then it went away."

The anxiety she started feeling was something she had never experienced before. She started to tell herself stories: "All that business success you have seen? That was just luck. You couldn't sell yourself out of a wet paper bag. You know that expertise you have had? There is no longer a market for it." Before long, her anxiety morphed into depression. She couldn't get excited about anything, let alone revive her struggling business. Soon she felt *nothing*.

About this time, Elise reached out to me to see if I could help her wife Karley turn around the business. I had met both of them a few years before at a business conference, and we had become good friends. I knew Karley had all the necessary elements to turn her business around, but we had to figure out why it wasn't working.

Our first order of business was to do some quick business triage and analyze exactly what was going wrong. We looked at Karley's financials and at her core marketing operations, including her business development, sales, and proposal processes. We talked about her mental models and current emotional state.

Our triage analysis revealed the first big gap: Karley had gotten so focused on the production of great work for her referred clients that she had forgotten to seed new opportunities in her network. She wasn't attending events, she wasn't connecting with partners, she wasn't sending newsletters, and she wasn't interacting with peers and clients on LinkedIn. Her clients, while extremely satisfied with the work she did for them, did not currently need any additional work. Her pond was all fished out.

As the business was sliding backward, she felt shame. She knew better! But still, here she was, feeling stuck.

Aware of her tender emotional state, I wanted to give her some easy and feasible wins. We started with a list of extremely small tasks, like sending a quick email to a past client to say hello or inviting a connected peer to grab a cup of coffee. I called them tiny marketing actions or "TMAs" for short.

While Karley was diligent and did her homework after each coaching session, she later told me this: "Because of the relationship that you and I had as good enough friends to be extended family members, I had a deep trust in you. But part of me was like, '*Really*, you are telling me that these little tiny actions are going to make a difference? Are you kidding me?'"

I wasn't kidding. Building a business is hard. Even if you have done it before, even if you have done it for years, there is always that pit in your stomach when you think: What if all of a sudden no one buys my stuff?

So many business owners are paralyzed by the process of finding customers because there are so many different ways we can reach them:

Do you call up old clients?

Start a Facebook page?

Write blog posts?

Send messages to people on LinkedIn?

Speak for free?

Put up a billboard?

Pass out flyers?

Cozy up to influencers?

Start dancing to nineties oldies on TikTok?

Tough love business influencers will tell you to hustle your way to building your own personal empire. I don't know about you, but I have no interest in building an empire. The last time I checked, empires were good for the very few people at the top, but they weren't much help to the many workers eking out tiny salaries while making empire builders rich.

What I want is a thriving ecosystem. I want plenty of money in my own pocket to pay bills and paint my walls new colors, buy new furniture, and take fun trips around the world with my husband and kids.

But I also want plenty of money in my employees' pockets, and in my clients' pockets, and in their neighbors' pockets, and in the pockets of every person walking down the street, and in the city and state coffers everywhere. I want software companies to have so much money that they build amazing tools that cut our working time in half. I want overflowing coworking spaces that incubate scores of new businesses that grow into thriving enterprises. I want busy Main Streets everywhere with happy people holding fresh cups of hot local coffee sitting outside of bustling cafés. I want community art nights and outdoor movies and restaurants with lines out the door. I want an abundance of creative writing and art and films. I want college students to have bustling side hustles and Internet entrepreneurs to hear the sound of their phone dinging with online orders. Is that just some pipe dream from my idealistic, raised in the 1970s, community-loving optimistic coach self?

I used to think it was. Until I started developing and applying a marketing model in my downtown Mesa community, impacting hundreds of entrepreneurs directly and thousands of their customers indirectly.

I used to think it was until I actively worked with business owners like Karley who found their business grew in direct proportion to their ability to connect to the ecosystems surrounding their ideal customers.

I used to think it was until I saw my clients' sales and profits accelerate quicker, more strategically, and with less frantic effort than espoused in the sleep-when-you-are-dead hustle culture.

The advice I share is not a hypothetical example based on a cool idea I had in the shower one day. It is based on decades of real work with real people. It comes from helping thousands of clients all around the world start, grow, and scale their businesses. I have spent the last six years codifying this approach into a method, testing it with entrepreneur groups around the country, with my clients, and in our own small business learning lab in Mesa, Arizona. I have watched it activate millions of dollars in sales, generate scores of partnerships, and strengthen the visibility and thought leadership of my clients.

The result is the *Widest Net Method*, or WNM for short.

This book teaches you the method, how it works, and how to apply it to your own business to activate a flood of new customers. While the focus of the book is on entrepreneurs and small businesses, the concepts apply to any size organization that's striving to develop deeper and more authentic relationships with their customers and to find new customers in places they may have never looked before.

If you are in corporate marketing, I particularly recommend the chapters on "watering holes," ecosystems, and partnerships. Identifying and working with others who are also striving to solve your customers' problem will expand your horizons and open up new business opportunities.

I am not going to make you read the whole book to understand the core ideas. Here are the highlights:

- Before you build a business, you have to make sure that it solves a problem worth solving, a problem that people will pay to solve, and a problem that you personally desire to solve.

- You have to know how to describe and recognize the specific characteristics of the perfect customer for your business.

- You have to craft offers your perfect customer can't refuse because they are the quickest, best, and most cost-effective way to solve their problem.

- You need to connect to the right "watering holes": places, in person and online, where thousands of these ideal customers hang out.

- You have to build relationships with them in a way that is respectful, inclusive, and that they don't find overbearing or creepy.

- As you build relationships, you need to demonstrate to customers that you are a smart, trustworthy person who has a unique approach to doing this work.

- You have to be really consistent with TMAs—small activities done consistently over a long period of time that generate leads and momentum.

- You have to know how to sell to these customers in a way that feels easy and aligned and valuable, to you and them.

- Over time as you scale, you need to build partnerships with trustworthy allies that allow you to grow without exhausting yourself in the process.

- And once you are in the admirable state of a well-oiled business with consistent leads of great prospects, you need to operationalize this marketing work, hire folks to work with you, and consistently plan ways to connect with new and interesting markets.

It sounds pretty straightforward, doesn't it? The process itself is not that hard to understand.

What you will find in each chapter is a specific way to craft your answers in a manner that is completely aligned with who you are and your own definition of success. If you follow the steps, you can be assured that your work will have deep meaning, create significant impacts, and literally transform the lives and businesses of the customers who work with you. And you can scale according to your own standards. As you take this journey with me, I will tell you this: there are no miracles. No one will do your work for you. But if you use the method, apply the lessons, and do the work, you will find yourself surrounded by cool partners, overflowing with opportunity, with a full client roster, taxes paid on time and in full, and bulging bank accounts.

As for our friend Karley? Within a year, she not only gained back her business to what it was preslump, she grew an additional 30 percent. As you will learn in the upcoming chapters, her rebound did not stop there.

Ready to begin?

THE
WIDEST
NET

STEP ONE:
FIND THE MISSION
AT YOUR ROOT

What are you willing to lay your body
down for, and say "Not on my watch?"
—Todd Henry, *Die Empty*

Whether you are a one-person startup or a mature business employing thousands, you must have a clear, compelling mission that drives everything you do—what I call your root mission. Finding your root mission can be challenging. Here's how I found mine.

I was presenting at a business conference and asked a simple enough question: "How many of you have ever seen a Native

American presenter at a business conference, speaking on a business topic?" I asked this question to the assembled group of entrepreneurs at Mothership Hackermoms, a coworking space in Berkeley, California. It was the very first stop on a three-month, 23-city tour speaking with business owners about ecosystem marketing. I asked the same question in 22 more cities, including New York, Boston, Washington, D.C., Philadelphia, Atlanta, Phoenix, Minneapolis, Sioux City, Fargo, San Francisco, and Vancouver, Canada. Twenty-three cities later, from a total pool of about 1,000 workshop participants, the sum total was . . . seven. And four of these sightings were from entrepreneurs in my workshop in Vancouver, Canada. What was the true problem?

The issue, as my husband, Darryl, and I discussed, was not that there were no Native American business owners. According to the US Census Small Business Survey for 2020,[1] there are an estimated 24,433 American Indian and Alaska Native–owned businesses with approximately $33.7 billion in receipts, an estimated 200,256 employees, and about $8.2 billion in annual payroll. Given that many smaller artisanal businesses and side hustles from Native employees are not reported, the number is likely much higher.

My husband, a Diné (Navajo) construction business owner for most of his career, had attended many business conferences in rooms filled with hundreds of Native business owners, who were experts in any specialty you could think of: accounting, graphic design, architecture, writing, software development, marketing, insurance, real estate, arts and crafts, and more.

The problem was, for very specific historical and policy reasons, these experts had next to no *visibility* outside of conferences specifically designed for Native entrepreneurs. Most organizers of mainstream business conferences, looking for diverse speakers, probably would not even consider looking for a Native American speaker because it just wasn't in their realm of experience. If they did consider it, they would have no idea where to look, since so few folks had taken the time to develop relationships with business leaders in Native communities or the Native employee affinity groups in larger companies.

My husband and I realized that our children, nieces, nephews, and extended relatives would have little to no chance of ever seeing a leader that looked like them and who lived in their cultural context speaking as an expert at a business conference—even though they clearly existed. If asked, the broader business conference audience would probably conclude that they never saw a Native American business expert speaker because there simply were no expert Native American entrepreneurs. Thus, a cultural stereotype is perpetuated. Pretty terrible, right?

THE PROBLEM IS EVERYWHERE

We also knew that the issue of lack of leadership visibility in our hometown of Mesa, Arizona, was not only a problem for the Native American business community, but also for many other historically marginalized folks like Black, Latinx, Asian, disabled, and LGBTQ entrepreneurs. In my 15 years of work building inclusive entrepreneur communities around the globe and talking to hundreds of partners who worked with small businesses, I knew that it was also a problem on Main Streets everywhere.

What could my husband and I do to help solve this problem, within our own span of control and resources, in our own community? How could we reflect on these lessons, codify them, and share them with our partners all around the country who were trying to do similar things? Our solution was to take a leap of faith.

We signed a five-year lease on a space right in the middle of Main Street in downtown Mesa with the purpose of providing a home base for our business by day and, on the weekends and evenings, providing a welcome gathering spot for many of the community leaders and business experts commonly overlooked or ignored to speak at and host business and cultural events.

Darryl named the physical space "K'é" (pronounced "keh" in English), which is a sacred Diné word that means system of kinship, connection, and belonging. We added "Main Street Learning Lab" to the name to make it clear that this art-filled, welcoming, bustling space right in the center of downtown Mesa was home to all kinds of testing, experimenting, and innovation.

Our goal was to highlight the leadership that exists within business leaders in marginalized groups who are rarely visible to the broader business community. By bringing together and providing a forum for a diverse range of business leaders, we intended to nurture opportunities for business deals, partnerships, and collaborations. Moreover, with the full talent of our leaders engaged, we were certain we could improve the business ecosystem in our local downtown Mesa community and beyond. And as we learned daily important lessons about building an inclusive ecosystem, I would apply these learnings to my business coaching models, trainings, and books.

We had found our mission. The next question was exactly how we were going to achieve our mission? Honestly, we had no idea. But we were determined to find out.

← ———————————— →

THE MISSION AT YOUR ROOTS

We spend inordinate amounts of time and money figuring out the *how* in our business. How do we attract customers? How do we create products? How do we build our operations? How do we hire and manage staff? How do we scale?

What most business owners fail to define in a deep and compelling way is *why* they are in business. Beyond making a profit, providing jobs, and contributing to the desired lifestyle of the owner, what is the reason you are in business? What concrete contribution does your business make to the world? A business that does not solve an important problem is not a business, it is a fad. You might ask, *What does defining my mission have to do with getting more customers? After all, that's why I'm reading this book.*

The answer is simple. Defining your overarching mission is critical for guiding the design, operations, and culture of your business—in other words, all aspects of your business. It is the foundation upon which you build your unique expertise, the value you bring to customers, and your thought leadership.

In addition, we live in a world of radical transparency. The internet provides a limitless forum for reviewing products, services, and companies. People communicate on social media. Word gets around faster than ever before. Eventually, your customers are going to find out exactly who you are. A company with a genuine, heartfelt mission that animates everything it does is going to connect with customers far better than an organization that is simply about making money or providing a nice lifestyle for the owners.

In my Widest Net Method, mission is the key to identifying numerous "watering holes" filled with ideal customers, identifying untapped markets where your products and services can be sold, and building partnerships that will increase your market reach and market share.

But perhaps most important, your clearly defined mission will keep you going when you are tired, when a client who owes you thousands of dollars is not returning your calls, when an unhappy customer roasts you on social media, and when your daughter is furious at you because you are always too busy working on your business to spend time with her. The mission of your business is your emotional fuel. It will help you answer the central question that shaped my last book, *Body of Work*: At the end of your life, when you look back at what you spent your time creating, will you be filled with gratitude or will you be filled with regret?

BACK AT THE LAB: LISTEN FIRST

We were crystal clear in our mission at the Main Street Lab: "nurture and highlight the leadership that exists but is rarely seen in our local business community."

But while we knew our mission, we didn't want to jump immediately into a program structure and design, because we had few relationships at all with the members of this community, beyond our family and friend ties. We needed to understand who these community members were, what was important to them, what problems and aspirations they had, and what would truly help them grow their businesses. So in our first year, we spent a lot of time in conversation with people in our community.

We soon learned, however, that some people really want to put you in a box when you are in the process of discovering a design that is truly aligned with the mission of your project. We had countless conversations that went like this: a person walking down Main Street would see the vibrant mural in our front window and walk through the door.

Person: "What is this place?"

Me: "We are a small business learning lab."

Person: "Is it a coworking space?"

Me: "Nope."

Person: "Is it a startup incubator?"

Me: "Nope, not exactly."

Person: "Do you [meaning me, Pam] share your expertise by teaching a bunch of classes?"

Me: "No, I don't."

Person: "Are you a nonprofit?"

Me: "No."

Person: "Well then what are you?"

Me: "We are not sure yet. We are waiting for our community to tell us what we need to be. What do you want us to be?"

This continued for a couple of years while we steadily increased the events led by experts from our Native American, Black, Latinx, and Asian communities, as well as other organizations serving these communities.

By the end of 2018, we were hosting events almost every evening and on the weekends. We had hundreds of diverse entrepreneurs each month coming from all over the greater Phoenix area to participate in programs led by leaders in the community. And businesses opportunities were growing, not because we imposed a top-down idea of what was needed, but because we followed our mission of simply supporting the leadership that already existed in the community but was rarely seen.

CREATING YOUR MISSION WITH THE WIDEST NET METHOD

If you want to build a legion of passionate customers, scale your platform, increase influence, or build a vibrant community of ecosystem partners, you have to be clear about why your business mission is important. The foundation for every audience-building strategy in the Widest Net Method (WNM) is a clear mission of your business.

We have all seen meaningless corporate mission statements that are so broad and generic that they don't evoke any emotion or action. As small businesses, we need to rehabilitate the use of a mission.

There are four critical principles to a WNM mission:

1. It Is Centered on Your Customers

Too many business owners think of their mission in terms of their own needs. They want to make a million dollars or generate recurring revenue so that they don't have to trade time for money, or they want to attract venture capital funding. These are business owner goals, not the mission of the business.

The mission of your business should be centered on the needs of your ideal customer (much more on this in Chapter 3).

2. It Is Deeply Rooted in the Problem You Are Solving or the Aspiration You Are Enabling

Sweetgreen, a restaurant with multiple locations around the United States, has this mission statement: "We believe the choices we make about what we eat, where it comes from and how it's prepared have a direct and powerful impact on the health of individuals, communities and the environment." With such a mission statement, Sweetgreen can and does provide many interesting ways to interact with their customers and fellow partners beyond just serving good tasting food in their restaurants.

3. It Is a Problem That Your Ideal Audience Views as Critical

It is not enough to be personally passionate about a mission. To have a viable business, you must have a large enough customer base who are willing to spend money to solve this problem.

Through market research and lots of audience analysis, you have to make sure that you are not pushing your random cool idea into the marketplace, but rather solving something deemed broadly valuable and important.

4. It Connects with a Deeper Root in You as the Founder

In addition to reaping the financial benefits of a successful company, founders need to be personally connected to the mission and root of their business. If you are going to spend years of your life working on, talking about, and thinking about solving the core problem in your mission, it better be worth your time, energy, and attention. When you feel an emotional connection and resonance with the work, you make sure that solving this problem is directly aligned with your top values, strengths, and skills.

MISSION POSSIBLE

Three years after opening the doors to K'é Main Street Lab, our mission was taking flight. We were collaborating with a vibrant, thriving community of Black, Indigenous, and people of color (BIPOC) entrepreneurs, and a rich ecosystem of partners including nonprofits, community organizations, government leaders, and academic institutions.

I was on an organizing committee for a Global Entrepreneurship Week event in downtown Mesa. Global Entrepreneurship Week is an event sponsored by the Kauffman

Foundation described as a "celebration of innovators who dream big and launch startups that bring ideas to life."[2] It takes place every November, with 2021 participation topping 180 countries and a total 40,000 events worldwide.

Eager to further our mission of increasing the visibility of Native American entrepreneurs, I suggested Violet Duncan for a panel discussion. Violet is an author, storyteller, educator, and performer (Native American hoop and powwow dancer). She's a proud member of the Plains Cree of Kehewin Cree Nation and Taino. I was excited to hear her unique perspective on entrepreneurship but didn't know any specifics of what she was going to share.

The morning of the event, our daughter Angie, who was 11 years old at the time, wanted to take a day off of school and go with me. This was the first time she had ever asked to attend a local event with me. She was a student in a very supportive Montessori program, so I knew her teachers would support her attending an experiential field trip. I said yes.

The morning of the event, Angie and I worked together to set up the tables, preparing for the 80 local entrepreneurs and community members attending from the greater Mesa area. The program was kicked off by an address from our Mesa Mayor John Giles. Then the panel began. Angie was sitting quietly and attentively listening to the speakers.

It was time for Violet to speak. She introduced herself in her own Cree language, in the way Angie has been taught to do in her Diné (Navajo) language since she was a little girl. Violet described her business and journey as a Native entrepreneur, with its highs and lows. Then she told a story.

When I was 11 years old, I attended the Canada Council for the Arts meeting with my mom. My mom is a dancer and an artist and was invited a few times a year to share her perspective of what artist representation looked like in Canada. While this was so important to her, the weeklong trips from our home in Alberta to Ottawa for the meetings made her terribly lonely.

So this trip I agreed to go with her to keep her company. At the time, I was not really interested in the arts, holding a long-burning passion for medicine. My dream was to go to medical school so I could find resources to support the health of the youth and elders in my community. I brought all my homework and tucked into a corner of the room where the meeting was taking place to get busy with my studies. I figured the gathering would be a bunch of people in suits talking about boring stuff.

When the meeting started, it was held around a huge round table and the artists were all different and interesting. Some of them had beautiful regalia on. I put my notebooks aside, and I asked my mom if I could sit at the table just so I could look at all the beautiful faces. She said yes, and encouraged me to talk and share my youth voice.

As I listened over the three days, the Canadian Arts Council continued to ask the meeting participants how they could bring the arts to the First Nation communities. After about three days listening at the table, I felt kind of brave.

"Let me say something here," I said. And then I told them that it's impossible to "find us on the rez." How *do you find that one arts kid on the rez in remote areas that are not even in a city or small town? They asked me, "Well, how do you see us approaching this?" And I was like, "Well, we need to be able to find a way to find you because you won't be able to find us. And they said, "OK, where will you find us?" "I don't know, I said. "I go to the youth center and I go to the after-school basketball and stuff like that." They said, "You are right, we are trying to find indigenous youth on the rez in the same way we reach youth in the densely populated inner cities. We need to change the way we think about this."*

A few months after this meeting, my mom shared with me that my questions led to a redesign of the Canada Council for the Arts website with a section designed specifically for indigenous First Nations people.

Before, the design and criteria were in no way aligned with how we viewed ourselves as artists. They finally understood that learning from elders is a form of education. They understood that we didn't learn to dance in a studio. They started to innovate outreach like paying dancers to go learn at a powwow.

My mom said "This happened because you were there. You let them know that they're not going to be able to find that one artist kid on the rez, that that kid needs to have easy access. We needed to hear your voice there."

She made me feel as if I did something that had a huge, a huge impact. I found out many years later that my mom had been saying the same thing for years, but until they heard me say it, they didn't really hear it.

While she was speaking, I looked around the room and saw everyone listening deeply and taking in Violet's words. I turned back to the front of the room and saw Violet lock eyes with someone and smile. I followed her gaze back to my table and saw she was looking directly at my daughter Angie, who was sitting proudly in her chair with a smile on her face, looking back at Violet.

My daughter Angie, also 11 years old, who had skipped school to attend an event with her mom, was hearing a powerful Indigenous woman entrepreneur tell her that her community had unique and valuable contributions and that young Native American voices mattered. The hair stood up on my arms and tears pooled in my eyes. Our mission was alive in this room.

EXERCISE: The Mission at Your Roots

1. What is the mission behind the work you do?

2. Why is it important to you personally?

3. When in your life, or in the lives of others you love, has the lack of this mission caused substantial pain or discomfort?

4. When in your life, or in the lives of others you love, has the presence of this mission caused substantial joy or freedom?

5. Imagine that your plan works, and a customer of your dreams has completely solved the problem that your

company is designed to solve. How would their life be different? What would they be able to do now that the problem was solved?

Finding your mission puts you on the path to building a great business. The next step is to identify the values that will guide your behaviors and actions and will keep you aligned toward building an organization that benefits customers, employees, and the world.

STEP TWO:
IDENTIFY YOUR VALUES

You don't have to look far to find companies that have committed egregious ethical violations. The business press is filled with stories of organizational leaders who defrauded investors, exploited their employees, or polluted the environment. Everyone has stories of companies they've worked for or did business with that violated their sense of right and wrong. A person who was terminated unfairly. Harassment that was covered up. Shoddy products that couldn't be returned. The list could go on. Is this who you want to be? Is this what you want your company to be known for?

Your purpose establishes what you're trying to achieve in your business and how you'll make the world a better a place. Your values are the beliefs, philosophies, and principles that drive your business. They are guideposts for the behaviors and actions—both large and small—that will enable you to achieve your purpose.

Business values allow you to define:

- Who will you and won't you do business with, and why?

- How you will make important decisions.

- What kind of culture will bring your mission to life?

- How you will choose the best partners to expand your business.

- Whom you will hire to work in your company.

- How you will conduct yourself in your business.

Common values include words like:

- Integrity

- Honesty

- Fun

- Trust

- Creativity

You can look for ideas and language for values in assessments such as the VIA Character Strengths at https://www.viacharacter.org/. If values expressed as singular words are not clear enough for you, you can use a tool called "Always and Never" from my friend and colleague Greg Hartle.

ALWAYS AND NEVER

Greg Hartle is an entrepreneur who has founded and sold multiple companies. He brings both a very pragmatic perspective to running a business, as well as a tremendous depth of perspective in the area of business ethics. I asked him how we translate general values like "fairness" or "honesty" into specific, behavior-based descriptions that let us know if we are putting our values into action.

One tool he shared was to create an Always and Never list for your business. As an example, in one of Greg's businesses, an Always is:

Any commitment made to a customer is always documented, shared with the customer, and signed off by a manager. This way we all know exactly what has been promised, and we will stop at nothing to ensure it is delivered.

The Nevers

Here are some examples of Nevers from business owners I work with:

Have early morning meetings.

Cancel a promise to my family to make money.

Make a promise that I know I can't keep.

Twist myself and my integrity in a pretzel to land a client.

Tell someone they can't make changes to their own website because they will screw it up.

The Always

And here were some examples of Always:

Let my clients know they matter, their life has purpose, and I value them.

Tell the truth.

Show up 100 percent intellectually.

Love them, and have fun!

Focus on solutions.

Choosing absolutes like always and never will force you to discern nice-to-haves from must-haves. You can say: "I will never work for a client who is unkind or disrespectful." Are you prepared to stand by this if you are about to lose your home and the only way to save it is by working with said unkind client? Are you prepared to stand by this if working with said client will lead to your lifelong goal of meeting and interviewing John Legend? (Not that I would know anything about that!)

The Hypocrisy Line

The examination of these always and never absolutes gets you bumping up against what Greg calls the "Hypocrisy Line." When you cross it, you violate your deepest ethics.

In my line of work as a career coach, I have met many, many people who have crossed over their Hypocrisy Line and are feeling the repercussions. Violating your sense of ethics knocks you off balance. It can make you feel scared or filled with dread. You may suddenly feel paranoid, like someone is out to get you. Or frequently, you feel dead inside.

The Power Is in the Examination

I have always had a hard time looking at life in absolutes. There are too many different angles and gray areas that can be driven by a range of different circumstances. Even in these shifting sands, there are some areas that you know deep inside are non-negotiables. Clarifying exactly what these are is the foundation of your organizational culture.

WHEN YOU REACH YOUR GOAL AND REALIZE YOU ARE OFF MISSION

Jeff Goins started his business with the personal mission to do work that lit him up and to share his personal and professional transformation in a way that was useful to other people.

A professional author, ghost writer, and writing coach, Jeff had built an impressive range of online courses and learning experiences, and his business was growing rapidly.

In the world of online businesses, reaching seven figures is an important milestone that many strive for. Who wouldn't want to share with the relatives at your holiday meal that the weird online business you gave up your stable corporate career to launch is now making a million dollars a year? That's what Jeff Goins thought as he diligently followed the advice of his entrepreneur buddies and his coach.

He had built a team and delegated much of his work to them. He had amped up marketing and lead generation activities. If he could just keep the grind going for another three to four years, he knew he would get to the magical place where he could let someone else run the business while he collected nice profits.

One morning while making pancakes for his kids, it hit him: he felt lost. Jeff described that time:

> I lost my way as an artist because I was trying to build something that was inauthentic to me. It had nothing to do with how much money I was making or how many people I was managing. It had to do with the intent behind my actions, which was I had this deep need in myself to feel significant. And I saw people all around me, including my friend Michael Hyatt, who was a mentor to me and who had spent 30 years ahead of me, building organizations and leading them. And I had this crazy idea, which was that I could basically do the same thing that he was doing.

The problem was, the specific activities Jeff was doing were not the things that made him interested in his business at all. He was managing subcontractors, writing email sequences, and obsessing over email open rates. He was not focused on the things he loved the most—diving deep into the writing process and teaching others how to do so.

Aside from the activities that were not energizing in his business, the financials were not rosy either. Even though his business was making over a million dollars a year, after team pay, business expenses, and taxes, Jeff's owner pay was closer to $80,000. Lower take-home pay is an understood part of the first few years of scaling a business, but it was painful to work so hard and see so little for his efforts.

Jeff realized that his path was not sustainable, because he was not building a business according to his mission or business values. He reached out to Seth Godin, who generously spent 30 minutes on the phone with him, laying out some options. Jeff said:

> Seth told me I could become a CEO and grow this into a real $50 to $100 million-dollar business that has the capacity to change the world. And if I didn't want to do that, I could make about $1.2 million dollars a year, have a handful of people to help me, pay my taxes and expenses, then with half of the money left over, put it in the bank and save it for the times when my art didn't make any money.

Jeff knew what he needed to do. He called his business coach to tell him that he was changing directions.

Over the period of about a year, he cut back his team, scaled back operations, and got back to doing the thing that got him into business in the first place: writing, and sharing his personal and professional journey in a way that would help others. Ironically, refocusing the business didn't impact his gross sales too much, but it did impact his profit: instead of bringing home $80,000, he was bringing home $600,000.

The transition was not easy.

It was really hard to tell valued team members that we were going in a new direction and I had to let them go. I also felt a little bit of shame among my other entrepreneurial friends who put in the three years of hardship to build their companies and now were living the easy life. But there was this immediate sense of relief, too, where I thought this was never right for me but it can be right for someone else. And that's OK.

Four years after his business pivot back to his roots, Jeff is building a new ghostwriting company and is actually excited about scaling it. This time, he is doing it on his terms, for reasons that are aligned with his mission and values.

EXERCISE: Define Your Always and Nevers

1. Take out a piece of paper or open a document, and create "Always" and "Never" columns.

2. List as many items as you can think of in each column.

3. Reexamine the list with the question: "Can I think of a valid exception to this rule?" If so, take it off the list.

4. Whittle down the list to those things that you feel are clear, feasible, and useful in guiding the direction of your business.

5. If you have a team, you can choose to do this process collaboratively.

6. Review your core list of projects, business operations, and marketing strategies.

7. Ask yourself "In light of my Always and Never list, do I need to make any adjustments in my business?"

8. Make adjustments.

9. Sleep better, and watch your business grow.

Now that your values and mission are clearly defined, it's time to move to the next step in the Widest Net Method that will change everything about the way you market and unlock countless opportunities for growth: defining the customer of your dreams.

STEP THREE:
DESCRIBE THE CUSTOMER OF YOUR DREAMS

*You will never win a sale if the only
things you know about your ideal customers
are that they are 45, make $100,000
a year, and drive a Subaru.*
—**Susan Baier,** Audience Audit

Karley Cunningham of Big Bold Brand from the Introduction was diligently doing her Tiny Marketing Actions (TMA) outreach and filling her journal with gold stars. Things were starting to move. She was having conversations with prospective clients again, and projects were rolling in.

But it still felt a bit haphazard. She was known for doing great general branding work, including company names, logos, full graphic design of materials, and website builds. But she still felt like her messaging was not quite right.

If you are multitalented like Karley, you can do a lot of things, so you say yes to a lot of things. Your clients know you do excellent work, but they don't necessarily understand what your "thing" is. You love your work but find that the process and outcomes of the work can change a lot depending on the type of client you are working with. You also struggle to describe what you do in a variety of settings, including networking events, where it is critical to have a clear and pithy answer for potential customers and partners.

Karley understood branding from a holistic perspective, including how it impacts marketing and sales, finance and accounting, HR, culture, production and distribution, operations, customer service, IT, and R&D. Business owners who use one-off solutions to building a brand end up with a chaotic, Frankenstein business presence that does nothing to position them in a crowded market.

Karley knew her approach was really different, but she needed a clear way to describe both her ideal customer for this work, as well as a succinct description of her core services so that the perfect kinds of prospective clients really understood what she did.

It didn't seem to matter the kind of industry her ideal customers were in, or their gender, or their location. It didn't make a difference if she called herself a "marketing expert," "branding expert," or "business consultant." How could she get her audience messaging right?

Ironically, the thing she did best for her clients escaped her when she tried to implement the same thing in her own business. She was too close to the process and couldn't see her own brand with objectivity and clarity.

LEADING WITH DEMOGRAPHICS

A common pitfall for many business owners is saying the market for their product or service is "Everyone! (with a pulse and a purchase order)." While it is true that the entire world may be better off with your coffee maker, productivity app, or coaching service, the reality is, it is impossible to market to "everyone."

Even when you have more specific data about the numbers of potential customers in your market, this does not mean you know exactly who you are looking to reach. Leadership consultants know the Fortune 500 generated 1.2 trillion dollars in revenue in 2020[1] and employed millions of people. Clearly there should be a small subset of these companies that have big problems you can help them solve. Website developers know 804,398 new businesses started in 2020,[2] each requiring a new website. If you just built five of these sites, you would meet your quarterly sales goals. Relationship coaches know there were 782,038 divorces in 2018. If you could reach 20 of those couples with your coaching before they hit the point of no return, maybe you could have saved them some heartache and lawyers' fees and filled up your relationship coaching for couples' retreats.

But how do you go from "oh my goodness, there are hundreds of thousands of people out there who could benefit from my product or service" to a real, paying customer with a pulse and purchase order? And once you close that business, how do you line up a bunch more behind them? It just takes a few minutes of staring into your computer screen trying to find "everyone" who could use your product or service before you realize it is impossible.

If you read any book or take an online class about marketing, they will usually tell you to start by defining an ideal client avatar. "Visualize the person," they say, "right down to what they are wearing."

You do your best to answer questions like:

- Where does she live?

- What kind of car does he drive?

- What type of aftershave does he wear? (Is it Old Spice Red Zone Aqua Reef or Old Spice Wild Bearglove scent?)

- How much money does she make?

- Do they wear white after Labor Day?

- Are their pants spun from organic or synthetic linen?

- What kind of flavor do they like in their lattes? Do they use almond milk? Are they lactose intolerant?

If you are like most of my clients, they have no idea how to answer these questions. Because demographics are the wrong place to start.

When I started my blog Escape from Cubicle Nation in 2005 (which became my first book, published in 2009), I thought I knew the profile of the person who might be attracted to it—young creatives earlier in their career who were not interested in slogging out decades in corporate life.

Over the last 10 years, as I helped thousands of people quit their corporate job to start a business, my audience ended up crossing just about every demographic and industry category you can imagine—from 75-year-old artists to 55-year-old software engineers to 30-year-old Indonesian hip hop artists. The core challenge they shared was desperately wanting to get out of corporate life and into their own business, without destroying their financial life in the process.

Before adding demographics to your ideal customer profile, you have to have a clearer way to understand which problems they are trying to solve; otherwise, you will waste huge amounts of time and resources spreading your message to a broad and generic market.

ATTITUDINAL SEGMENTATION

I struggled to help my clients describe their ideal clients until I met marketing consultant Susan Baier, an attitudinal segmentation researcher with her firm Audience Audit.

Susan helps marketing agencies and their clients know their best prospects, create compelling content, and attract more customers using her proprietary research method. She developed her approach with her sister Sarah McKenzie, who holds a PhD in statistics, out of frustration with generic marketing advice, like "Know your audience, then develop your marketing content around that profile." The problem was, Susan found, everyone skipped the step of telling you exactly *how* you were supposed to know your audience.

Susan begins with an approach to audience segmentation that focuses on the audience's problems, and a specific survey method that marketing agencies and their clients use to understand the underlying problems, concerns, and attitudes of their ideal customers. From this research, they develop targeted and effective marketing campaigns that speak directly to the needs of their audience. This approach is critical in framing the first part of the Widest Net Method, because to know what kinds of products or services to create, and the complementary services that surround it in the ecosystem, you must define your audience by problem, challenge, or aspiration.

Case Study:
Why Are Your Customers in Business?

To understand this approach a bit better, take a look at a case study from one of Susan's past clients. Keap (formerly known as Infusionsoft) is a software as a service (SaaS) customer relationship management (CRM) sales and marketing platform for small business owners. In 2014, they commissioned Susan and Audience Audit to do an audience survey to figure out the motivations and characteristics of their core audience segments. This research was used for marketing campaigns, as well as for thought leadership.

The audience segments they discovered from the research were the following four categories:

Passionate Creators start their business because they love what they do. They believe in their product or service.

Freedom Seekers value having the ability to control their own schedule, career path, and environment in which they work. They desire independence and flexibility.

Legacy Builders are more likely to have started a business with a family member and see it as a practical economic choice. They care about securing their future.

Survivors embody the reality that sometimes running a business is scary, even more so than it is rewarding. Despite this, they are determined to succeed.

Because each of these four different audience segments are driven by different attitudes and motivations, they care about different product features and marketing messages.

If your core marketing message to Freedom Seekers is to invest a huge amount of time and energy into their craft, that message would not resonate. They aspire to Tim Ferriss's four-hour workweek[3] and want to be hanging off a zip line in Costa Rica while passive income flows into their bank account. Conversely, if you try to tell the Passionate Creators that by automating their marketing functions, they can just sell online products and not ever have to have any customer interaction, they are likely to respond negatively. Passionate Creators love their work and long to spend time with their clients in weeklong retreats where they dig in and do deeply transformational work. Their goal is to deepen their craft, not necessarily to spend less time working.

Customers in each of these attitudinal segments can look very different demographically. Which is why Susan cautions you against leading your ideal customer description with a demographic description of your market like, "Women, between the ages of 45 and 55, who make $100,00 a year and drive a Subaru."

In this case study example, two 55-year-old women could fall into very different attitudinal segments, and your messaging would miss them if you catered only to their age.

PROBLEMS

As I do with many of my clients, I recommended that Karley work with Susan Baier so she could really hone and focus her ideal client profile and have a clearer way to describe what she did.

As Karley and Susan began to dig deeper into the audience work, they explored in great depth the kinds of challenges Karley's ideal customers were experiencing

- Their marketing wasn't working.

- They were not attracting enough business.

- Their brand wasn't resonating, clear, or needed work.

- They were not sure how to differentiate themselves from competitors.

- There was a lack of team alignment and direction.

Through analysis, Karley and Susan discovered that all of these problems are actually symptoms of the same problem, which was that they lack clarity on the fundamental beliefs and truths of their organization and do not have one core strategy.

With this insight, Karley repackaged the process she had used with clients over the years into the Surefire Method,™ a system that gets to the root of the problem that manifests all of the symptomatic challenges that get in the way of a business's growth. Using this method, Karley defined her ideal customers this way: motivated business leaders who were specifically seeking a strategic advantage and desired bold differentiation.

The Surefire Method weeded out prospects who just wanted a pretty website, a nice-looking logo, or who saw branding as a color palette and a snappy tagline. It attracted prospects who knew that if they wanted to stand out in a sea of sameness and get world-class results, they had to examine every part of their business in building their brand. And they needed a specific method and an experienced partner to lead them in this process.

By focusing on leaders who wanted bold differentiation, Karley had found her people. And those people were about to find her in a big way.

DEFINE YOUR IDEAL CUSTOMER

Are you ready to define your ideal customer? Let's examine the four key steps in Susan Baier's Audience Audit process:

1. Define your ideal customer(s) in terms of their problems, challenges, or aspirations.

2. Add relevant demographic information to each audience profile.

3. Define the qualities and characteristics of people you want to work with and the people you don't want to work with.

4. Build an upside/downside decision matrix to qualify prospects.

You'll examine each of these steps in detail, and then you can fill out the exercises in this chapter.

Step 1: Define Your Ideal Customer by Problem, Challenge, or Aspiration

The first step in defining your ideal customer in useful terms is to define them according to problems, challenges, or aspirations they have. You already have a big head start: the core problem or aspiration you defined in your mission in Chapter 1 is the starting place for the added detail you will flesh out in defining your ideal customer profile.

Here are some examples of how different businesses could define their ideal customer profile by the specific problems their ideal clients face or the aspirations they hold:

A landscaper: "I help homeowners who want to showcase a beautiful yard, while maintaining value in their home, but who don't have time to do yard work themselves."

A consultant: "I help organizations save money by automating their most repetitive tasks."

A jewelry maker: "I help people display a unique and bold sense of style that makes them stand out in a crowd."

Step 2: Add Demographic Information to Your Ideal Customer Description, Where Relevant

In some cases, adding demographic information to your Ideal Customer Profile will sharpen your marketing message and increase its effectiveness. You remember in Chapter 1 that the entire mission of the K'é Main Street Learning Lab was focused on highlighting the leadership of Native American and other entrepreneurs who are often invisible in most mainstream business events. These demographics are a critical part of achieving our mission, so they are important to add.

Depending on the nature of your business and your specific goals, you can add some of the following demographic filters to get clearer about your ideal customer profile.

Examples of Demographics

- Geographic location

- Income level

- Education level

- Race or ethnic origin

- Age, gender, or sexual orientation

- Type of business

- Number of employees

- Annual sales

- Industry

Here are examples of ideal customer profiles with demographics added:

> **A landscaper:** "I help homeowners **who live in planned communities of more than 100 homes in Austin, Texas,** who want to showcase a beautiful yard, while maintaining value in their home, but who don't have time to do yard work themselves."

> **A consultant:** "I help **health care organizations with 500 employees or above in the San Francisco Bay Area** save money by automating their most repetitive tasks."

> **A jewelry maker:** "I help **female African-American business owners** display a unique and bold sense of style that makes them stand out in a crowd."

The Power of a Clear Shift in Audience

Michael Margolis is the CEO and founder of Storied, a Los Angeles–based strategic messaging firm. I spent some time with Michael in 2015 at the beginning of his self-described "walkabout," a yearlong journey working remotely around the world while he reflected on the next stage of his body of work. He attended the Vancouver, Canada workshop of my 23-city tour teaching entrepreneurs about ecosystem marketing, the early testing grounds for the model in this book.

At the time, Michael had built a successful range of training offerings housed in his Story University. His market was mostly independent consultants and solopreneurs. While he loved his customers, this business to consumer (B2C) audience required a huge amount of effort, energy, and resources for marketing, because he had to amass a pretty large customer base to generate a decent profit.

On his walkabout world tour after the workshop, spurred by thinking about who his truly ideal customers would be, Michael reflected on his work with innovators and change agents. In the B2C market, you might get the occasional person who called themself a disruptor or change agent, but who was likely an author or consultant looking to jazz up their LinkedIn profile. These folks were rarely part of an organization or institution.

Michael discovered that the world of innovation and design thinking had made significant leaps from when he had first encountered it in the early days of 2006 and 2007. He realized that design thinking was how the future was getting built, especially inside the most innovative technology companies in the world.

Michael began to shift his audience focus to a business to business (B2B) market, with the heads of product management as his ideal customers. He discovered that people in these roles were literally building the future, but in many cases were struggling to communicate their vision to their own companies, as well as to the rest of the world. His method of storytelling was a perfect fit in this environment.

Michael's new focus began to take flight, and soon he was working with some of the most innovative companies and organizations in the world. Storied's clients now include Facebook, Google, NASA, Hulu, Bloomberg, SAP, Greenpeace, and more. In Michael's case, the core method of his work didn't change, but the audience for the work did—and that had a profound impact on the scope, depth, and financial returns generated by his company's engagements.

←——————————→

Now it is your turn! Let's dive into an exercise to help you define your Ideal Customer Profile by the problems, challenges, or aspirations they hold.

AUDIENCE AUDIT EXERCISE:
Problems I Solve

This exercise helps you identify problems that real people struggle with (whether as part of their job or personally) and that you might want to solve.

Different people might need to accomplish the same thing, but they often have different reasons why they haven't accomplished it already. One person may not have the money; another may not have the time; a third may not have the right resources in place; and a fourth may not know where to start looking for the help they need (or even know that it exists).

Each of these would be a different problem, and each would probably have a different solution. Don't worry too much about describing these people based on demographics or the companies they work in. (In fact, if you can do this exercise without mentioning demographics or company characteristics like industry and so on, even better!) Focus for now on the problem they're having, why they haven't solved it already, and how you can help.

Create a general problem-based description of your ideal customer profile, then create specific marketing campaigns for demographic segments.

I help people who need to	They haven't solved this problem already because	How I could help them solve it

Reviewing the preceding list, are there are any relevant demographic characteristics that you want to add to your profile, to fully accomplish your mission? Think about things like:

- Of all the people in the world I could help with my product or service, who would I feel great about helping? (Add demographic information related to a person's identity, circumstance, or lived experience.)

- Am I passionate about building a local business, or do I want to build a national or global business? (Add demographic information about your local town or city.)

- Given the focus of my product or service, would any specific geographies be more attractive than others as a market focus? (Add demographic information including a list of cities, regions, or states that would be the best places to target for your marketing and advertising.)

- Is this product or service relevant to people who come from a particular set of beliefs? (Add demographic information about political or religious affiliation.)

- Is this product or service a best fit for companies in a certain financial situation? (Add demographic information about annual sales or profit.)

- Is this product or service a best fit for companies with a certain scope or scale? (Add demographic information about number of locations or employees.)

Step 3: Define the Qualities and Characteristics of People You Want to Work with and the People You Don't Want to Work With

Even when you have a clear idea of the kind of problems you want to solve for your ideal customer, you still need to define the affective characteristics of people who would be ideal to work with. Affective characteristics are interests, feelings, and attitudes people use to navigate personal and professional environments. For example, the affective characteristics of an ideal client for an accountant who works with business owners who need to organize their finances may be a person who has a willingness to develop new habits and an excitement to learn new financial skills. A nonideal client would have the opposite characteristics: resistance and a bad attitude toward doing the work.

Because every business owner is different, you get to define what you consider positive and negative characteristics of your ideal client.

WHO DO YOU WANT TO WORK WITH?

Think about the characteristics of past clients who you have worked with and list the behaviors you do and do not want to support in your business.

My ideal client has the following characteristics:

My nonideal client has the following characteristics:

Step 4: Build an Upside/Downside Decision Matrix to Qualify Prospects

It is not possible to meet all the needs of your ideal customers. There may also be some customers who you think are lovely people but are not ideal fits for your offerings. This Upside/Downside exercise from Audience Audit will help you plan for sales and qualifying conversations.

AUDIENCE AUDIT
EXERCISE: Upside/Downside

Review your customer problems exercise from earlier in the chapter.

This exercise helps you place yourself in your audience's shoes and to understand from your audience perspective what it would be like to work with you. It is for your eyes only—no one else ever needs to see it.

First, identify which audience you're using this worksheet for.

You should do one of these for each of the audiences you're exploring, but don't try to combine multiple audiences on one sheet. You want to focus on the upsides and downsides of a single audience at a time.

In Box 1, list things these audience members will love about you—your expertise, your understanding of their situation, your pricing, the way you work—whatever.

In Box 2, list things you love about this audience—the characteristics that make you love working with them.

In Box 3, list things they might worry about relative to you. For example, pricing or if you're inexperienced in something that's important to them—whatever might concern them. These are things that will keep them from working with you if you can't change them or eliminate their concerns some other way.

In Box 4, list things that make you reluctant to work with them. Focus on things they can't fix and things you can't get over.

From This Audience's Perspective . . .	From My Perspective . . .
1 I'm ideal because . . .	**2** This audience is ideal because . . .
3 I may not be ideal because . . .	**4** This audience may not be ideal because . . .

Armed with this upside/downside information, as we get to later chapters that outline specific marketing strategies and tactics, you can develop useful resources and information to qualify ideal customers, address any of their concerns or reservations, and ensure that you are only marketing to the people you love to serve and you can truly help with your product or service.

A NOTE ABOUT JOB TITLES

Even after clearly defining their ideal customer profile, many business owners get obsessed about what to call themselves.

"But am I an entrepreneur or the head of a social enterprise?"

"Should I call myself the CEO or Chief Awesome Officer?

"I am a consultant, but sometimes I also coach as part of my consulting. So, am I a coach-sultant or am I a consultacoach?"

I wish I were making these up.

It is handy to have a title. You often need to provide one on your social media and speaking bios and when you are introducing yourself around a business networking table. The title itself rarely does anything to tell prospective clients or partners what you can actually do for them. But if you combine the title and a problem-focused audience description, this makes your introductions much clearer.

EXERCISE: Fill in the Blanks

I am a ___*(fill in business title)*___ and I work with ___*(fill in type of client)*___
who are trying to ___*(fill out type of problem you solve)*___.

Here are examples of how the structure would work
with real people:

**"I am a (marketing consultant) and I work with (authors)
who want to have a successful book launch without
spending too much time, money, or unnecessary
energy."**   **(Tim Grahl)**

**"I am a (data scientist) and I work with (other data
scientists) who are trying to increase equity in data
science."**   **(Heather Krause of We All Count)**

**"I am a (professor and author) and I work with (leaders)
who want to lead authentically and inspire meaningful
engagement.**   **(Brené Brown)**

READY FOR THE NEXT STEP

Clearly defining your ideal customer profile with the tools in
this chapter will unlock tremendous opportunities in your business. It is the key to the entire Widest Net Method.

When you center on the core challenge or aspiration of your
ideal customer, then you can define exactly what they need to do
to solve the problem, which will give you their customer journey
and offer a map (which you are jumping into in Chapter 4).

Once you have the customer journey, you can decide which things you actually want to do in your business and which things you can refer out to your other ecosystem partners (which Chapter 5 covers). This is vitally important because the fastest way to lose momentum in your business is to try to solve every problem your customers have.

Follow the process outlined in this chapter, and you will no longer have to shout into the void of the Internet with the hope of finding someone brave enough to work with you. You will be well on your way to envisioning and connecting with thousands of ideal customers.

STEP FOUR:
THE OFFER THEY CAN'T REFUSE

*The key to evangelism, sales, presentations, and
now ecosystems is a great product. In fact, if you
create a great product, you may not be able to
stop an ecosystem from forming. By contrast,
it's hard to build an ecosystem around crap.*
—**Guy Kawasaki,** Chief Evangelist for Canva

Password software around the world is clogged with logins
for online classes purchased in a moment of adrenaline
and hope. "Maybe this class will be the one to make me get
my life and business together," pine online course purchasers.

After a week of furiously watching videos and downloading worksheets, most online learners lose interest and turn to the next great thing that is certain to make them healthy, wealthy, and wise. Research proves that hardly anyone finishes an online course after they buy it. *Inside Higher Ed* research found that only 6 to 7 percent of online learners complete an online course.[1]

Wes Kao has spent six years trying to hack this statistic. After building the popular altMBA course with Seth Godin in 2015, then doing the same thing for other thought leaders like Outlier.org, Morning Brew, and Professor Scott Galloway's Strategy Sprint among many others, she knew there was a very specific need in the market for cohort-based courses:

> *The completion rates for online classes were super low, because people would enthusiastically sign up for a calligraphy hand lettering class or a music class or a sales class, and a tiny percent would actually finish it. This wasn't fulfilling the promise that online education was supposed to be.*

When Wes and Seth designed the altMBA, they wanted to try an entirely different approach and experimented with the idea of "what if we didn't have lectures and we had group projects instead; what if instead of everything being loose and optional, deadlines were mandatory, meeting times were synchronous; and instead of doing it by yourself, you're doing it with a bunch of people around you that were handpicked and curated and on a similar level of commitment as you are?"

Through this experimentation, they inadvertently created the category of cohort-based courses. This category of cohort-based learning is growing because people are catching on to the fact that people were never meant to learn by staring at a screen and sitting for long periods of time. It is a very unnatural way to hold anyone's attention.

Through her research and experience with clients, Wes also saw that the technology, tools, and processes required to put together a cohort course was still really, really rough.

It was basically stitching together free or low-cost tools for video conferencing, class hosting and inter-class communication as well as email and calendar invites. There was not a single place where a student could have a seamless experience in a native culture-based course built entirely around what that experience is. Paying for all these platforms is expensive and unwieldy.

So Wes and her cofounders Gagan Biyani (the cofounder of Udemy and founder of Sprig) and Shreyans Bhansali (the cofounder of Socratic [sold to Google] and first engineer/employee at Venmo) raised $4.3 million with First Round Capital and are building a company named Maven with a new product to streamline the process, remove the slog, and streamline the administrative logistics of what it takes to design, build, and execute cohort-based courses that students will actually finish.

Their vision goes beyond an excellent learning experience.

We are building something that will democratize who gets to share their knowledge in a cohort-based course and get paid for it. Not every course creator can afford white glove level

consulting. Our product will make best in class course cre-
ation accessible to anyone with valuable knowledge to share.

At the heart of their startup is a fierce focus on the customer journey and the student experience. They aim to make the overall learning environment as ease-filled and integrated as possible.

YOUR CUSTOMER'S QUEST
FOR A SOLUTION

Now that you have done the homework from Chapter 3 and know the specific kinds of problems you want to solve for your ideal customers, you are ready to design the perfect product, service, or offering.

To understand what you could sell your customers and the other ecosystem partners who are also helping them solve their problems, you need to understand the bigger picture of what is commonly described as a "customer journey." This journey takes your ideal customer from where they are today to where they want to be when their problem is completely solved.

What is really important to understand is that to know the specific help you will provide to your customers through a specific product or service, you need to know *all* the steps they need to take and the obstacles they need to overcome to achieve their goal. For example, software company Intuit's mission is to "Power prosperity around the world."[2] Most business owners are familiar with their flagship products Quickbooks and TurboTax. What do Intuit's customers need to "power their prosperity?"

They have to travel a transformational journey from struggling to pay bills to financial abundance.

To do this, they need the following things:

- They need a well-paying job or successful business.

- They need to know how to manage the money they earn.

- They need a range of bank accounts, including checking and savings accounts.

- If they have had a rough journey with money in the past, they need skills to effectively manage the money they have, as well as skills to strengthen their money mindset.

- They need to understand how credit works and how to improve their credit score.

- They need investment accounts to grow the money they have and the knowledge to choose the best investment vehicles for their particular situation.

- As their own wealth grows, they may need advice on how to choose charitable organizations to donate to or social enterprise companies to invest in.

- And they definitely need some accounting and tax software to help them easily track income and expenses and comply with the regulations that govern our tax systems.

Intuit's products fit at particular stages of their customers' transformational journeys from financial stress to prosperity. But they are not the only products or services that their customers need to reach their mission. Choosing the exact part of the customer journey where your product or service fits is the key to creating the perfect offering.

AUDIENCE FIRST

Brian Clark knows a thing or two about building successful companies. His journey as entrepreneur started in 1998. A lawyer by training, he was an early adopter in using email newsletters to market his business. He then moved into real estate and began to build out websites to promote his business. "I worked in pretty traditional industries, but I understood SEO, landing pages, email, and content. What was innovative about my work was the way I attracted customers."

In 2006, he started a site called Copyblogger on the premise that he no longer wanted to work with individual clients. He wanted to share what he learned about generating business leads through what is now called content marketing. His focus at first was simply building an audience. He did not start out of the gate with paid products because he wanted to pay very close attention to what his audience responded to and wait for them to tell him what they needed. "We take that approach as pretty common-sense knowledge these days. In 2006, it sounded truly radical. But it makes sense, right? Shouldn't you look for signals for pain points and desires that people have as opposed to dreaming up a product and hope that people buy it?"

For the first year and a half, Brian built the Copyblogger audience and tested for product interest with some affiliate promotions. Affiliate promotions are great for market research, because people will tell you all day that they're interested in buying your product, but until they pull out that credit card or open their wallet, you don't know for sure if they will actually do it. Brian and his team conducted some tests to validate certain hypotheses about what their audience needed. That led to their first product: an online course.

Copyblogger's humble beginnings were not an indicator of future growth. Brian and his team went on to build a whole series of successful courses, membership programs, and eventually WordPress themes, generating eight figures a year. Brian sold the StudioPress division to WordPress Engine in 2018 and sold the Rainmaker division in 2019. Now he is working on two new projects: Unemployable, a site focused on seven-figure companies that don't require investors or employees, and Further Consulting, a site focused on health, wealth, and personal growth for people in their forties and fifties. From his experience building multiple audience-first businesses, Brian recommends this:

- Start with an audience that you serve strategically, and pay attention to their needs and opportunities.

- Find ways to make money rather than rush.

- Once you are ready, develop your first product or service.

- Document your operations and processes.

- Trust that your audience will tell you what they need, and it is your job to create it correctly.

STARTING WITH YOUR FIRST OFFERING

Wes and her team at Maven are dealing with the issue that all new ventures face: how do you design your first product without spending too much time, money, or energy on research?

Their approach is aligned with those in the lean startup methodology world, which is to build a minimum viable product, or MVP. In an MVP:

> *The first step is figuring out the problem that needs to be solved and then developing a minimum viable product (MVP) to begin the process of learning as quickly as possible. Once the MVP is established, a startup can work on tuning the engine. This will involve measurement and learning and must include actionable metrics that can demonstrate cause and effect question.*[3]

Wes and her team know they don't have to have their entire customer journey figured out before they begin inviting people into the product or service.

Wes says: "Each time we build something, we jump in and look for patterns. We fix things that inhibit a great experience. With everything that we do, including our first client classes, we improve the baseline, and remove things that don't work."

Communication with your clients is essential, especially in the early stages. You can build mini feedback loops as you test each new thing, then make tweaks if they tell you that your communication wasn't clear, or a step was clunky or unnecessary.

It is not easy to roll out an offering that is not perfect, but Wes offers this counsel for new entrepreneurs: "Trust yourself that it will be helpful. Codify as you go. Soon, you will have a rough customer journey, and can focus on making changes and improving as you go."

THE FOUR PARTS OF BUILDING AN OFFER

Creating an offer your ideal customer can't refuse, and is actually willing to pay for, is a four-part process. I use the term *offer* to describe both a physical product and a service, knowing that many entrepreneurs have a combination of both.

Part 1: Define the Transformational Journey

When you sell a product or service, your customer is not just purchasing a "thing," you are leading them on a transformational journey:

- They have a starting and ending point where they go from feeling stuck, stopped, or overwhelmed with their problem to fully solving the problem.

- They go from not having enough customers to pay their bills to a full and overflowing customer roster and plenty of money in the bank.

- They go from not being able to sleep due to back pain to a pain-free night with full back mobility.

- They go from desiring a beautiful home interior but having a small budget to living inside a bright and renovated home, while maintaining their budget.

What does it take to get them fully across the bridge of transformation? That is your task to define.

The source of context for the transformational journey is the combination of your mission and your ideal customer profile. Your mission defines a big problem or aspiration in the world that your business is designed to solve (or at least solve part of it). Your ideal customer profile tells you the specific kind of person you want to work with and the more granular problem your product or service is solving.

To pick up on our Intuit example, their mission is to "Power Prosperity." The specific product promise for their product Quickbooks is to "Save time, track money and get important insights."[4] In this case, you would be leading your customer from being a stressed-out disorganized mess, with receipts all over their desk, unreconciled bank accounts, and no idea of the current revenue, expense, and profit numbers in their business, to a confident and prepared business owner who can tell you exactly how much money they made last month, last quarter, and last year, and the right kind of business intelligence to make smart spending and saving decisions.

Part 2: Diagnose What Is Preventing Your Customer from Solving Their Problem

To come up with an offer that will both attract the interest of and actually solve the problem for your ideal customer, you have to diagnose all the things that are preventing them from successfully solving the problem.

The obstacles fall into these four categories:

1. **Knowledge, skills, or information.** What specific things does this customer need to understand, or what do they need to be able to do to solve this problem?

2. **Thoughts.** Which unempowering or destructive thoughts are inhibiting their ability to take action and make the transformation they have signed up for?

3. **Tools.** Which tools, frameworks, or methods are needed for them to solve this problem?

4. **People.** Which kinds of people are needed to help them solve this problem? (This can include professional service providers, peers or partners.)

EXERCISE: What Bothers You the Most?

Entrepreneur Greg Hartle, whom we met in Chapter 2, suggests that an easy way to figure out how to design an offer is to ask your customers: "What bothers you about

(fill in the blank with the problem you are trying to solve)?"
Listen closely, then ask a lot of follow-up "why" questions.

For example, if you want to solve the problem
of teaching your ideal customers how to take action
marketing their business, you might ask the question:
"What bothers you about taking action to market your
business?" They might say things like:

- There are too many choices of places to market,
  and I don't know where to start.
- I feel like a slimy salesperson if I reach out to a
  prospect I don't know.
- I am terrible at video, and everyone tells me I
  need to make videos to market my coaching
  business.

With each answer, ask follow-up "why" questions, like
"Why do you feel like a slimy salesperson?

With this information, you can think of ways to
eliminate, improve, support, or streamline these
bothersome things.

Part 3: Design the Offering That Is a Fit for You and Your Business and Refer out the Rest

Even though I don't know you or your business, it is safe to say
that you don't have every single skill, resource, tool, or answer
to completely solve the problem you want to solve for your ideal
customer.

To completely solve their problem, they may need:

- Software

- A specialized professional

- Freelance workers

- Inspiration and motivation

- Financing

- Specialized supplies

If you try to design your business to deliver every single one of these resources, you may grow into an unwieldy and unprofitable organization.

If you are a consultant:

- Do you really want to build your own app, or partner with a company that has already built one?

- Do you want to hire a large staff of specialized professionals and freelancers, or refer this work to a specialized agency?

- Do you want to produce all the inspirational and motivational content for your ideal customers, or refer them to excellent podcasts that do it for you?

As you will find out in the next chapter on ecosystems, you may lose a tremendous amount of value and momentum in your company if you try to do everything yourself. Instead, ask yourself:

- Of all the things our ideal customer needs to completely solve their problem, which can (my team) and I do the best?

- Which parts of this customer problem are too expensive to solve ourselves?

- Which parts of solving this problem require our specific point of view and/or lived experience?

Part 4: Engineer the Steps Leading up to and Away from the Offering to Create an Exceptional Customer Experience

When our son Josh was ready to get braces, I was referred to a place called Macdonald Orthodontics in Mesa, Arizona.

From the outside, it was nothing special. It was housed in a typical tan building in a strip mall a half a block from my kids' junior high school. I was not yet sure that we wanted to get braces for our son, but I thought we could check it out and see if we liked the place. Then once we made sure we had the budget, we could see when to get the braces.

From the moment we stepped in the door, the customer experience began. The receptionist was friendly and welcoming. The forms were ready to fill out with a fresh pen.

We were greeted for a tour by a very friendly assistant who walked us through the building. The space was clean, well-designed and well-lit. She pointed out the soft-serve ice cream machine that patients could use immediately after getting their braces tightened, piquing the interest of our teenager. She brought us into a room with comfortable chairs for us and a reclining chair for Josh. It looked out over a beautiful mini garden.

The dentist came over and did the exam right away. After the exam, while the x-rays processed, we moved to the next room where we watched a video about different types of teeth and jaw situations requiring braces. The dentist came in shortly with the x-rays and showed us exactly what needed to happen to straighten Josh's teeth.

Then they went over the financials. There was a simple financing process that just required the first month's payment of $166 that first day. "Do you want to get the braces put on today?" they asked.

I was kind of shocked. I had expected that we would have to schedule a follow-up appointment, always a difficult thing to do with two busy working parents and a kid in school. We looked at Josh. "Do you want to get your braces on now?" He said yes.

The entire experience was perfectly designed for my needs. And clearly it worked. Not only did Josh get his braces from Macdonald Orthodontics, but our daughter Angie did too. I recommend them to other parents all the time, because of their excellent customer care and intelligent offer design over the entire customer journey.

ENGINEER YOUR OWN EXCEPTIONAL CUSTOMER EXPERIENCE

As you design your own offer, examine each part of your business operations that your customers will need to interact with to receive it.

- Marketing

- Sales

- Scheduling

- Payment and billing

- Email communication

- Shipping (if relevant)

- Customer service

- Tech support

Greg Hartle suggests that you examine friction points through your customer journey communication. Pay close attention to unnecessary gatekeepers, the duplication of requests (e.g., having to fill in the same information multiple times on your website), or inconsistencies in response time.

The most important thing, Greg says, is to be *congruent*. Customers will pick up immediately and intuitively if your behavior changes as they move through their customer journey with you. Do they have the same feeling when they interact with your website as they do when they call you on the phone? Do they have the same feeling about you once they start working with you as they did when you were courting them in the sales process?

Never stop improving your customer journey operations and communication.

OFFER OR PRODUCT FUNNELS

Very often, when you are designing an offer for your business, you also need to design ways to attract ideal customers to this offer, as well as nurture them into deeper engagements or follow-on services. The design of this structure in the internet marketing world is commonly called a product funnel, and it is a helpful way to organize your marketing and sales communications.

There are many very specific marketing, sales, and product funnels from companies like digitalmarketer.com or Hubspot. You can select the specific model that fits your business. Regardless of the model you choose, you need to answer these five questions.

1. **What are the free ways to attract the attention and interest of our ideal customers?** (videos, blog posts, social media stories, free speaking, etc.)

2. **What could I trade for an email address?** (e-books, free tastes, digital downloads, or checklists, etc.)

3. **What is a low-cost offer to let my ideal customer develop a working relationship with me?** (onetime event, short coaching or consulting engagement, short paid online course, etc.)

4. **What is my primary offer?** (The main and most profitable offer that is designed to solve the exact problem you love to solve for your ideal customers.)

5. What are follow-up or deeper ways my ideal customers can work with me? (longer-term engagements, annual programs, follow-up memberships or masterminds, etc.)

As you build out the marketing for your business with the Widest Net Method and begin to seed new opportunities, you want to make sure that you have your offer funnel filled out. You can always swap out marketing assets or featured products once you gather feedback from your market.

Offer Funnel Example: The Home Edit

As a certified home organizing show addict, I was so excited to learn about the Home Edit. Founded by two lively business partners, Clea Shearer and Joanna Teplin, their company organizes homes in a signature clean and color-coded style. Their Instagram account has amassed 5.2 million followers, helped by their exquisite branding, great photography, and friendship with famous customers and fans like Reese Witherspoon.

Here are the ways their products lay out in the product funnel structure:

Free Level

Instagram: @thehomeedit

Netflix special: *Get Organized with the Home Edit* (free to those with a Netflix subscription)

Email Trade

Pop-up on their website invites you to be notified first about new product releases, offers discounts and promotions on products.

Low-Cost Offering

They have a range of organizing products, some catalogued to their individual Netflix episodes.

Primary Offer

The Home Edit likely makes more money with products than services, but you can also hire their extended team to come to your home to organize a room for you.

Follow-up or More Expensive Offers

If you have a larger budget, you could hire the Home Edit team to organize your entire house. It would be a color-coded dream, but it doesn't come cheap.

Now it's your turn to summarize your thinking about an offer for your ideal customer. In upcoming chapters, you learn how to position and sell your offer, connect with ideal partners, and deepen your thought leadership.

EXERCISE: Dream Customer Offer

The mission of my business is to:

My dream customer, defined by their problem, challenge, or aspiration:

To solve this problem, what state are they going from, and what are they going to?

From:

To:

For this customer to completely solve their problem, what are all the steps they need to take? (It might be easiest to first do this as a mind map, then place each item in the most logical order.)

Step 1

Step 2

Step 3

Step 4

Step 5

Step 6

Step 7

Which of the preceding steps do you want to address with your product or service?

What can we do exceptionally well?

Briefly describe your product or service, and which step(s) they correlate to.

Which steps will best be handled by a partner or referral?

EXERCISE: Simple Offer Funnel

What are the free ways to attract the attention and interest of our ideal customers? (videos, blog posts, social media stories, free speaking, etc.)

What could I trade for an email address? (ebooks, free tastes, digital downloads or checklists, etc.)

What is a low-cost offer to let my ideal customer get a sense of working with me? (onetime event, short coaching or consulting engagement, short paid online course, etc.)

What is my primary offer? (the main and most profitable offer that is designed to solve the exact problem you love to solve for your ideal customers)

What are follow-up or deeper ways my ideal customers can work with me? (longer-term engagements, annual programs, follow-up memberships or masterminds, etc.)

Wes Kao and her team at Maven have modeled how to develop your offer in the context of a big and important problem worth solving and iterate the product design and customer journey as you roll it out.

This next chapter illuminates, in ways you may have never imagined, multiple gathering places, what I call "watering holes," where you can connect with thousands of ideal customers who are eager to purchase your product or service. You're just getting warmed up.

STEP FIVE:
THE WATERING HOLES WHERE THEY GATHER

*Do you already know that your existence—
who and how you are—is in and of itself a
contribution to the people and place around
you? Not after or because you do some
particular thing, but simply the miracle of
your life. And that the people around you, and
the place(s), have contributions as well? Do
you understand that your quality of life and
your survival are tied to how authentic and
generous the connections are between you and
the people and place you live with and in?*

—Adrienne Marie Brown, *Emergent Strategy:
Shaping Change, Changing Worlds*

n June of 2020, a headline flashed across Bob Moore's phone and he knew one of his most serious business missteps had been finalized: Google had purchased Looker for $2.6 billion.

Bob, before founding his current company Crossbeam, had cofounded RJMetrics, a main competitor to Looker in the business intelligence space. While he admired the product and team at Looker, he was disappointed in the outcome, since his company had all those things plus a four-year head start.

He ultimately sold RJMetrics to Magento in a modest transaction that was orders of magnitude away from the $2.6 billion windfall earned by Looker. What was the difference between the two companies? Reflecting on what happened in a blog post, Bob said:

> *You could point to a hundred things, but if you dig deeply enough one core product decision is at the root of most of them: Looker placed itself at the center of a massive ecosystem, while RJMetrics operated as a silo. They made other products more valuable, and we were where your data went to die. What felt like a strategic advantage—we were a one-stop shop, the only thing you would need— ended up being our downfall.*
>
> *I learned a hard lesson: your place in an ecosystem of tech partners is just as important, if not more so, than the quality of your product itself. Marc Andreesen was right when he quipped that "software is eating the world." But in today's marketplace, ecosystems are eating software.*
>
> *I'll never make that mistake again.[1]*

Like Bob Moore reflected about his experience with RJMetrics, software as a service (SaaS) companies know that the key to their survival is narrowing their product niche and growing market share through building partnerships with other companies that share customers. Bob's new venture, Crossbeam, is built around this premise, acting as data escrow for SaaS companies who seek opportunities to collaborate, comarket, or partner.

Software companies are not the only ones that are organizing their business models around ecosystems. Michael Margolis, CEO of Storied in Los Angeles, reminded me that many different industries use the interdependent, ecosystem model by different names. He said, "In the nonprofit world, they call it collective impact. In the world of biopharma, it's about industry collaboration. In other areas like enterprise manufacturing, it's open innovation."

Ecosystem has become a buzzword in economic development circles as well. The Kauffman Foundation, an organization that funds nationwide entrepreneur development, has built extensive toolkits for cities across the nation, like their Entrepreneurial Ecosystem Building Playbook 3.0.[2] In all these environments, companies understand that the key to their success is deliberate interdependence.

So why don't more small business owners gravitate toward ecosystem models for their business models?

EMPIRE WORSHIP

In the entrepreneurial world, we love hyperbole.We fashion our-selves kings, queens, moguls, and mavericks. We want to crush, dominate, hustle, and grind our way to the top of a mythical empire and sip champagne while sitting astride a lion.

There is only one problem with this model. If you have any kind of ambitious mission, it is impossible to accomplish it alone. The most successful entrepreneurs understand that their power lies in their ability to identify, build relationships with, and eventually partner with other players in the ecosystem.

We have been made to believe that it is quaint to focus on "building community" with people outside of our immediate customer or prospect circle. What a nice thing to do when you have leisure time, right? We also describe our ideal customers as "targets" and other service providers in the space as "competitors" (and often enemies). Empire language is focused on control, competition, and domination. While excellence in your own field and ownership for your results is a critical part of running a business, thinking you have to position yourself as the lone expert in your market will shrink your opportunities and narrow your audience.

Our mission is to solve the core problem faced by our ideal customers. And we cannot do it alone.

SMALL BUSINESS OWNERS AND ECOSYSTEMS

There is nothing I have seen that helps business owners grow more strategically and quickly than looking at their marketing through the lens of an ecosystem. For the purpose of this model, I will first define the terms *ecosystem*, *watering hole*, and *thought leadership*.

An ecosystem is composed of all the services, products, organizations, events, and media who are aligned with your values and that provide your ideal client with the complete set of tools, resources, and information to solve their problem. Your ideal customer is at the center of the ecosystem.

Within this ecosystem, there are "watering holes," which are places, in person and online, that congregate multiples of your ideal customer in one location. Examples of watering holes include associations, events, podcasts, popular magazines, "best of" lists, and online groups. The organizers of these watering holes share a mission with you: to solve the core problem of your ideal client.

Thought leadership is simply your specific point of view about how to solve the problem defined in your mission and ideal customer description. To be a valuable member of an ecosystem, you need to provide some unique perspective, method, process, or approach that is a valuable and necessary part of solving the problem.

To illustrate with a specific example, a business attorney serves a greater mission of mitigating the risk and protecting the assets of business owners. Specific ideal customer problems or aspirations this business attorney could provide include:

1. Ensure their clients have a solid legal structure in place to prevent being sued.

2. Build a legal foundation for the businesses to allow scalable growth and sales to happen.

3. Research and protect core brand identity and naming to ensure the brand can grow without risk of violating trademark protections of other business owners, which would require rebranding and rework.

For the audience problems defined by our hypothetical lawyer, ask the following question: Who else helps businesses and brands to grow and scale?

- Business coaches

- Bookkeepers

- CPAs

- Marketing experts

- Sales experts

- Copywriters

- Financial planners

- Video producers

- Graphic designers

All of these professionals may be working with your ideal clients already in their area of expertise.

Next, you identify a watering hole for any one of the preceding professionals, like AICPA, which is an association of CPAs with over 400,000 members. With such a connection, you could offer a professional development workshop about legal issues facing businesses at AICPA's annual conference, exposing you to thousands of potential referral partners.

Then you could identify a similar watering hole for each of the other referral partners—business coaches, bookkeepers, marketing experts, sales experts, copywriters, financial planners, video producers and graphic designers. Your same professional development workshop could be tweaked slightly for each audience and pitched to each vertical. Now add a few additional connections, like identifying the top podcasts that serve each of these partners. What if you could be a guest on these podcasts, sharing your valuable point of view and helping their clients to successfully grow? What if you then identified the top software used by each of these partners and developed some content for the software company to share on their own channels as part of their content marketing strategy?

You can see that with just this initial short list of potential partners, you are already generating a lot of very efficient, one-to-many points of connection where you are sharing your message with ideal referral partners. As you walk through the step-by-step process of identifying your ideal ecosystem partners and watering holes, you will find that you don't have to connect with every single partner to build a robust marketing plan. You will use filters and discernment to discover the most effective and fruitful relationships. In each of these places, you are playing a specific role of, first, finding people who offer complementary services for your ideal audience, and second, providing your tools, point of view, and problem-solving approach to help your ideal customers grow.

Let's look closer at 10 segments of what I call the Ecosystem Wheel, which are specific places where you can find watering holes and partners.

THE 10 SEGMENTS OF THE ECOSYSTEM WHEEL

The Widest Net Ecosystem Wheel is divided into 10 distinct segments that represent overall sectors to look for people who also draw or attract your ideal clients. To be the right fit for your business, they should also share core values and support your mission.

They are:

1. Service providers

2. Thought leaders/influencers

3. Associations and clubs

4. Faith communities

5. Media hubs

6. Events

7. Nonprofit organizations

8. Governmental institutions

9. Academic institutions

10. For-profit companies

FIGURE 5.1 The Widest Net Ecosystem Wheel

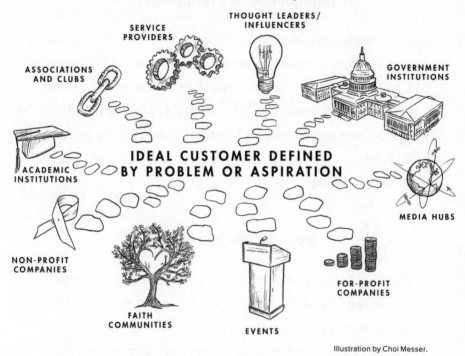

Illustration by Choi Messer.

Here are the segments of the Ecosystem Wheel with examples.

Service Providers

Service providers provide a complementary service to your exact ideal customer. Their service is critical for your ideal customer to completely solve their problem. If you are a graphic designer working with a business owner, your ideal customer likely needs a photographer and a copywriter to completely solve their problem. If you are a wedding planner, your ideal client also needs an event planner, makeup artist, photographer, and caterer.

Thought Leaders/Influencers

Thought leaders are experts in the fields critical to the success of your customer. Some might be in your direct field of expertise, and others in a complementary area of expertise. From a traditional lens, some could be viewed as your competitors. Your ideal customers are likely following their work, liking their posts, reading their books, watching their TED talks, and listening to their podcasts.

Associations and Clubs

Associations are amazing watering holes for ideal customers. They are organizations focused on a specific profession for the purpose of professional and personal development. Many have publications, conferences, and member directories. There is even an Association of Associations (ASAE: The Center for Association Leadership at https://www.asaecenter.org/).

Clubs are very similar, but they can be organized around more personal fan topics. These could be celebrity fan clubs, athletic groups, or local civic organizations like the Rotary Club.

Faith Communities

Faith communities are important gathering spots where their members learn more about their religion or tradition, pray, and share fellowship. Increasingly, they also are places that provide a much broader array of supportive services like parenting, marriage, finance, and business support.

Media Hubs

Media hubs include all the places where information is professionally written, recorded, or shared. They include television, radio, newspapers, magazines, podcasts, blogs, and social media. Depending on the audience you are trying to reach, you may target them differently.

Events

Live events gather people under a theme and main promise. They include attendees, speakers, producing partners, media partners, and sponsors.

Virtual events, which became very popular during Covid-19, can also be extremely powerful. They include the same players as live events. But connecting with people in a virtual event requires more preplanning, research, and follow-up, since you don't have the luxury of bumping into someone in the hallway and having a great spontaneous conversation.

Nonprofit Organizations

Nonprofit organizations are mission-based organizations designed to solve a particular social problem. They come in all shapes and sizes, and some have significant financial resources.

Governmental Institutions

Governmental institutions are funded by public dollars and include staff and departments covering a wide range of topics and services, including economic development, health and human services, and many others. Local governments often partner with businesses on specific initiatives, lending their reach and communication access to their residents and constituents.

Academic Institutions

Academic institutions, especially at the college level, have a variety of departments charged with doing deep research in many areas related to business. They also have career programs for students and adult education departments for the general public. Increasingly, they are partnering with businesses to develop civic projects, joint ventures, and incubators.

For-Profit Companies

For-profit companies sell a product or service to your ideal client. They can be small mom-and-pop shops or large multinational corporations. Larger companies are connected to thousands and sometimes millions of customers that can be an ideal fit for your product or service. They also partner with experts, thought leaders, and influencers to produce marketing content for their customers.

THE ECOSYSTEM OF SHAME AND VULNERABILITY

Brené Brown is a powerful example of leveraging the depth and breadth of her ecosystem to share her body of work. Her research on courage, shame, and vulnerability at the University of Houston inspired her first book, *Women & Shame: Reaching Out, Speaking Truths & Building Connections*, published in 2004. She couldn't interest an agent or publisher, so she borrowed money and self-published. Three years later, Penguin bought the self-published book and changed the title to *I Thought It Was Just Me (But It Isn't)*.

In 2012, despite her own hesitation and vulnerability, she delivered a TEDx talk in Houston that changed the trajectory of her career. Catapulted to stardom with millions of views of her 2012 talk, everyone suddenly became aware of the power and universal appeal of her message.

She has since written five straight *New York Times* best-sellers, starred in a Netflix special, and applied her work in the most unlikely of places, including the CIA, Stanford Business School, Facebook, Google, West Point, the Seattle Seahawks, and Southwest Airlines. Even the Happiest Place on Earth (Disney) recognized they couldn't fulfill their mission without understanding shame, vulnerability, and courage.

In addition to Brené's (prepandemic) full speaking schedule, she has trained service providers in her method through her rigorous licensing and certification programs. Her partners include:

- Social workers

- Teachers

- Business and life coaches

- Consultants

- Human resource executives

- Sports coaches

From the sample of her client list, you can see how Brené has personally shared her work in just about every segment of the Ecosystem Wheel and built the capacity for others to amplify it in their networks, communities, and organizations. Now with a top-rated pair of new podcasts on Spotify, *Unlocking Us* and *Dare to Lead*, she has beacons to ensure her point of view and problem-solving content travels far and wide across the world.

DISCOVER THE ECOSYSTEM OF YOUR IDEAL CUSTOMER

Using watering holes within an ecosystem designed to solve your ideal customer's problem is a strategic, efficient, and effective way to build your business. Leveraging places, in person and online, where someone smart and wonderful has already taken the time to cultivate a vibrant community, and who is, by definition, interested in your expertise, will save you time in the long run. As you build your own body of work, you will develop a beacon to attract your own community, a topic that I will thoroughly discuss in Chapter 7.

Now it's time to get down to the serious work of discovering the ecosystem of your ideal customer. This will be an ongoing, iterative process that will eventually be operationalized in your business, as covered in Chapter 10.

In ecosystem mapping, there are four phases: review, research and evaluate, connect and track, and streamline and operationalize.

Phase 1: Review

All the work you have done so far in earlier chapters is the foundation for building an ecosystem map.

- Review the mission and values you crafted in Chapters 1 and 2.

- Review your definition of your ideal customer, based by problem or aspiration, from Chapter 3.

- Review your customer journey map from Chapter 4 to see all the steps this ideal customer needs to take to completely solve their problem.

Phase 2: Research and Evaluate

There are three steps to research and evaluate your initial ecosystem list.

Step 1: Empty Your Brain

Using the preceding information, go through the Ecosystem Wheel and list which individuals, events, or organizations might also share the mission of solving the problems of your ideal customers. Because this list is likely to grow, you may want to organize it in a spreadsheet divided into the different Ecosystem Wheel segments (there is a workbook for this at https://pamelaslim.com/thewidestnet).

Don't be surprised if you don't have a lot of ideas in the first pass, because if you have never thought about this before, you may not have been paying attention to other ecosystem partners.

Step 2: Ask Three Favorite Customers

After you do your first pass based on what you know, select three of your ideal customers (or people who fit the description of your ideal customers) and ask them these five questions centered around the problem you solve for them in your business:

1. What was the most helpful book you read that helped you solve your problem?

2. What kind of software or products do you use ("in your business" where relevant, or "to solve your problem" in the case your business is in another area, like health or personal finance)?

3. What was the best event you ever attended and why?

4. What publications (magazine, blog, or newspaper) do you regularly read? Who is your favorite columnist?

5. What other service professionals or businesses do you work with besides me?

If they are willing to spend more time with you, you can ask them questions about resources they use to solve their problem around the entire Ecosystem Wheel.

Try to talk to ideal customers from as broad a demographic range as possible, since some of these people may have connections to communities and watering holes you are not familiar with.

The first five questions will give you a lot of information you can use to fill out your Ecosystem Map.

Step 3: Research the Contacts and Expand Your List

An easy way to expand your ecosystem reach is to take the initial list of watering holes or thought leaders and research the connections they have. For example:

- At your ideal customer's favorite conference, who were the other speakers? Who were the sponsoring companies? (You can find this information easily by going to the event website. There usually are tabs with information about the speakers and sponsors.)

- Research an interesting looking speaker from that event, and write down other events where they have spoken. (Many speakers list their events on their speaking page, or if they work with a speaker's bureau, you can see references there.).

- If you have some of your ideal customers' favorite thought leaders on the list, go to the library or bookstore and see who endorsed their book on the front and back covers. Add these names to your thought leader and influencer tab (as long as they align with your values).

- Go to Amazon and look up your thought leader books. You will see the "Products related to this item" (that are paid sponsored ads, which means someone took the time to target your like audience) and "Books you may like."

- Install a link-tracking tool like Evernote or Pocket on your browser, and create categories that correspond to the Ecosystem Wheel. When you come across an interesting article, bookmark it and tag it with that topic. On a weekly or monthly basis, review your articles and add any interesting watering holes or potential partners to your ecosystem spreadsheet.

Phase 3: Connect and Track

Once you have a healthy list of ideal customer watering holes and partners, you want to create an initial Seeding Plan (don't worry, this is detailed in Chapter 6). In this plan, whittling down from your big list on the spreadsheet, you will create a short list of:

- **Media hubs** you are interested in being featured in (magazines that could feature your story, podcasts to be a guest on, guest posts to write on a blog, etc.).

- **PB&J partners** to connect with because they offer highly complementary services to your ideal customers.

- **Online groups** to join that are filled with ideal customers or partners.

- **Associations** that have members interested in your content.

- **Events** that would be ideal for a speaking gig (virtual or in person).

From this short list, create a Seeding Plan, which will make it easy for you to reach out and make an initial connection with these potential ecosystem partners.

These small seeding plans will form the basis for your tiny marketing actions (TMAs) that you will take consistently over time and will eventually streamline and operationalize (which are covered in detail in Chapter 10).

Phase 4: Streamline and Operationalize

Over time, you will identify key marketing activities that drive consistent results and constantly put you in front of new audiences. At this stage of business development, most business owners do one or all of the following:

- Hire team members to support the research, partner outreach, and systemization of marketing content.

- Implement technology tools that help automate and streamline activities, without sacrificing the human touch of the Widest Net Method.

- Partner in bigger ways with ecosystem players to create cobranding, sponsorships, and comarketing activities.

Because it takes time and effort to get the ecosystem mapping and marketing operations in place, it is essential to streamline and operationalize whatever you can so you don't spend all your time in research mode.

HOW DO YOU USE ECOSYSTEM DATA?

The biggest advantage to having your ecosystem list is that it has been expressly created around the mission, values, core problems, and aspirations of your ideal customers. Instead of spraying your marketing messages randomly in the big universe of the Internet, you are choosing places that are likely to connect you with multiples of your ideal customer. You can use this data to:

- Select audiences for paid ad campaigns.

- Select ideal sponsors for you own event or podcast.

- Find great referral partners (what I call PB&Js).

- Conduct book launches.

- Recruit team members.

- Create your marketing content calendar.

- Find guests for your podcast.

Case Study: Ecosystem Recruiting in Healthcare

One of the best use cases for the ecosystem model is in recruiting.

André Blackman, founder and CEO of Onboard Health and one of *Forbes' 40 Under 40* leaders in healthcare, got tired of hearing that there was a "pipeline problem" for diverse talent in the field of healthcare. He started his blog Pulse + Signal in 2009 and wrote about the intersection of public health, technology, and inclusion.

As a natural inclusive network builder, André knew a tremendous number of diverse experts in the healthcare field, but many organizations were not connected with this talent. Because healthcare directly impacts every member of society, it is important to have diverse employees working at all levels of healthcare organizations.

In founding Onboard Health, André uses his powers of connection to both identify watering holes and key partners who have relationships with great diverse talent, as well as understand how to prepare organizations to create more inclusive and equitable environments so people from diverse backgrounds feel good joining the organization. Here is a sampling of his ecosystem partners, past and present:

- **Event:** The Aspen Institute Ideas Festival/The Aspen Institute (https://aspenideas.org)

- **Thought Leaders:** Katie Drasser, CEO of rockhealth.org, Veni Kunche, founder of diversifytech.co, Dr. Bernard J. Tyson, former chairman and CEO of Kaiser Permanente (he passed in 2019).

- **Media:** Sherelle Dorsey, CEO of The Plug (https://tpinsights.com/), a publication that examines changes in technology and business sparked by Black ingenuity, Afrotech (https://afrotech.com), a news site for "all things Black in tech."

- **Academic institutions:** UC San Francisco, UC Berkeley, University of Maryland School of Public Health.

- **Referral partners:** Assessment professionals; diversity, equity and inclusion strategists; career coaches, executive coaches

- **For-profit businesses:** Blavity, Inc., a diversified digital media company that builds platforms to inform, entertain, and engage communities of color.

André says, "We are living in a time where authenticity is important. I started building community first, then experimented with some consulting projects, which eventually led to the creation of Onboard Health. I would not have gotten a clear idea of what was needed, nor would I have been able to achieve the success we have made as an organization if we didn't focus on building community first."

Finding Interesting Ecosystem Pairings

Think of some word associations for *summer.*

Grass: cartwheel.

Barbecued chicken: corn on the cob.

Front porch: ice cold lemonade.

Some things just go together, like my husband's favorite sandwich, peanut butter and jelly, otherwise known as PB&J. These natural pairs are so complementary that when you think of one, you can't help but think of the other.

Part of developing an expansive ecosystem mindset, especially if you sell an idea, rather than a service or a product, is to revisit your ideal customer profile from Chapter 3 and determine what kinds of product- or service-producing businesses could use your ideas. Some creative "unusual pairings" examples include:

- Shonda Rhimes' *Year of Yes* book and Peloton series. Taking inspiration from Shonda Rhimes' *New York Times* bestseller, fitness company Peloton created an entire series of classes that took core concepts from the book and used them as inspiration on the rides. Themes included self-care as a form of activism and unlocking the unknown.

- When I worked with Susan Cain in the early stages of building her Quiet Revolution (quietrev.com), she partnered with office furniture maker Steelcase and used the research and ideas from her *New York Times* bestselling book *Quiet* to create the Susan Cain Quiet Spaces furniture, a line designed to cater to introverted workers who do not thrive in loud open space environments.

- Martha Stewart and Snoop Dog have become regular collaborators on projects such as VH1's *Martha & Snoop's Potluck Dinner Party Challenge.*

Take inspiration from these unusual pairings to imagine your own creative ecosystem collaborations.

CROSSBEAM MISSION, VISION, VALUES IN ACTION

Learning from his past mistakes, Bob Moore and his team at Crossbeam center collaboration, partnership, and ecosystem development in everything they do. The business model is built on specific values of collaboration, as you can see from their mission, vision, and values:

OUR MISSION

To create a more connected business world by powering the exchange of data between companies.

OUR VISION

To transform the way all companies partner by building and leading an invaluable new class of software.

OUR VALUES

Trust is our business: We create value by building trust in our company, our team, our technology, and our network. Never let anything compromise that trust.

FEED THE NETWORK

Our customer network is our most valuable asset. Prioritize its growth.

EQUITY

We will build a workplace that ensures everyone access to the same opportunities to share in our success.

THIS IS FUN

Few people are lucky enough to do what we do. Follow the fun in every step of the journey.

Rather than creating a place where "data goes to die," as Bob jokingly referred to his past startup, Crossbeam is now the "LinkedIn for data," facilitating new partnerships and comarketing opportunities on a daily basis. Sean Blanda, the director of content at Crossbeam, produces top-quality materials to help new customers navigate the tricky process of evaluating and building trust with new partners.

Their ideal customer is a director of partnerships at an SaaS company who is responsible for finding partners to expand their customer base. Sean says "Partner Managers are more relational in general, given the nature of their job. People work with people who are enjoyable to work with, and who truly care about what they do. We get to facilitate the old school Internet ethos, which is all built around equality and pitching in."

Crossbeam's partners are benefitting from their business model, evidenced by testimonials like this:

Wordpress VIP:

Crossbeam has been indispensable to us at WordPress VIP over the past 12 months as we've updated our Technology Partnership program. Their account mapping tools have given us lightning-fast insight into mutual customers and prospects when we're considering new partners. And their team has been flexible and thoughtful, consulting us

*on product planning and actively collecting our feedback,
then quickly turning around new features that solve real-
world business challenges for us.*[3]

Zendesk[4]:

*We used Crossbeam to create a list of our prospects over-
lapped with our partner's customers. We then narrowed
down the ones we wanted to talk to and now we have
those introductions all teed up for the next quarter. If you
speak to sales reps in dollar signs, they will listen. That's
what Crossbeam allows the partnerships team to do.*

*It's validating to see the number of overlaps we have
with a partner and realize we should be working with
them more. We weren't able to do these things without
Crossbeam because we didn't have the data, I didn't have
the time to manually sift through the data for 100 partners. Our partnerships used to be one-sided. But now, our
partners can easily loop us into new opportunities. As those
deals close, I can start to think about justifying more head-
count for partnerships. I was flying blind before Crossbeam.*

EXERCISE: Create Your Ecosystem Map

My business mission (from Chapter 1):

My ideal customer, defined by problem, challenge, or
aspiration (from Chapter 3):

My customer journey steps (from Chapter 4):

Instructions: Go through each of the sections of the Ecosystem Wheel and note specific people, places, organizations, or watering holes that would be good connections to reach your ideal customers. You can track your ideas in a mind map or spreadsheet (for a spreadsheet template, go to https://pamelaslim.com /thewidestnet).

1. Service providers

2. Thought leaders/influencers

3. Associations and clubs

4. Faith communities

5. Media hubs

6. Events

7. Nonprofit organizations

8. Governmental institutions

9. Academic institutions

10. For-profit companies

After you do your first pass based on what you know, select three of your ideal customers (or people who fit the description of your ideal customers) and ask them these five questions centered around the problem you solve for them in your business:

1. What was the most helpful book you read that helped you solve your problem?

2. What kind of software or products do you use ("in your business" where relevant, or "to solve your problem" in the case your business is in another area, like health or personal finance)?

3. What was the best event you ever attended, and why?

4. What publication (magazine, blog, or newspaper) do you read on a regular basis? Who is your favorite columnist?

5. What other service professionals or businesses do you work with besides me?

Update your spreadsheet with this information, and prepare for your Seeding Plan in Chapter 5.

PREPARE TO SEED

Now that you have a starter list of watering holes, in person and online, where you could potentially reach multiples of your ideal customer, you are ready to develop a deliberate, relational, and consistent plan for building connections.

It is normal to feel a little uneasy and overwhelmed with this part of the method, since you are moving from hypothetical research to real, live human connections. Don't worry—I will give you multiple ways to ease into getting to know people in your ecosystem, and form relationships in a way that doesn't feel transactional or overbearing. You may be surprised at how fun it is to meet people who share your mission and passion for solving your ideal customer's problems.

Let the opportunities begin!

STEP SIX:
THE SEEDS YOU PLANT

*Though I do not believe that a plant will spring
up where no seed has been, I have great faith
in a seed. Convince me that you have a seed
there, and I am prepared to expect wonders.*

—**Henry David Thoreau,** *The Dispersion of Seeds*

I hopped on Zoom with my new client, Heather Krause, a data scientist in Toronto, Canada, who had spent her 20-plus year career working globally with national governments, transnational corporations, and the largest players in the non-governmental organization (NGO) space. Heather explained that she wanted to build We All Count, a project with the mission of creating equity in data science. She said:

In my 20 years in the field of data science, I had seen many individuals being negatively affected by poor research practices. Secondly, I could absolutely see from all of my work that an orientation towards data was only getting stronger, not getting less. I also knew that the people who were trying to do mission driven work with data were trying their hardest to do good, but their good intention was being accidentally misdirected into harmful practices. I knew that changing these practices in our field would make a huge difference to individual lives of very oppressed, marginalized people.

After creating the foundation of her digital platform by reserving the We All Count URL and setting up a basic website, she started to build her methodology, publish articles, and gather resources. Her audience was growing, but very slowly. So I shared the Ecosystem Wheel and she researched watering holes and thought leaders who were also committed to solving the same problem. Once this was done, I suggested she reach out to the thought leaders she discovered, introduce herself, and learn more about their work.

Heather says this now about the homework assignment:

I was crystal clear on what I needed to do to build my method from a technical perspective. But I had no idea how to do it from a human perspective, like how to have an awareness-building conversation with these people I didn't know. I had no experience even being part of a

community, much less creating a community. This is
because I had been actively making sure that I was never
part of a community for two decades.

A self-identified big introvert, she continued: "I want to be sure you understand how much I did not want to build community. If I went to a Starbucks and they started remembering my name, I would go to a different Starbucks, even if it was ten blocks further from my house."

Given her mission, there was no way around identifying and building relationships using her Ecosystem Wheel if she wanted to build a large audience for her work. We started slow. "Just start with a request for a 15-minute get-to-know-you conversation," I said, thinking it was a simple and straightforward request. She bit the bullet and reached out to a few people on her list. They agreed to meet for 15 minutes on the phone.

After she conducted the first few conversations, we had a coaching call. "How did it go?" I said with a smile, expecting to hear things like, "Wow, the time flew! It was so easy; I am not afraid to do the calls anymore!" Instead, she said this: "The phone calls were a disaster. They were not a success. I was terrible at them. It was like going on a blind date with somebody that I'm sure was sending themselves fake text messages to make an excuse to leave."

"I need you to give me some really concrete structure," she said. "Can you give me a template for exactly how to conduct these calls?" It was then I realized that some of the communication structures I took for granted were not evident to everyone.

Of course, that made sense. I spent my entire career building community and teaching people how to build relationships. But not everyone had shared my interest or inclination to nerd out on such things. Heather and I started to break down this process into specific steps. And the results were pretty amazing.

YOUR SEEDING PLAN

There comes a time in every client's journey where they realize that all the conceptualizing, planning, and strategizing about building an audience needs to end and a process of connecting with real, live humans needs to begin. This can bring up uncertainty, insecurity, and terror. A lot of the terror, in my opinion, comes because of the way we have been socialized to think about "business networking," which is often taught in an extremely transactional way.

Real human relationships are clumped together in abstract terms like, "You need a bigger platform if you want to sell more stuff! You have to increase your mailing list! You need higher numbers!" I get it. Everyone knows how math works. The more people you have on your mailing list when you launch your book means more people who can potentially buy it. The more people you have following your Instagram posts about fashion, the higher number of sales you are likely to make from the shopping links you include in your posts.

But it's easy to forget that each one of these "numbers" is a real person who is connecting with you out of choice and vulnerability. They are trusting you with their email address or sharing your work with their friends and colleagues. This business relationship is a human relationship, and it does not defy the norms of how we make good decisions about the kind of people we want in our life.

Many people resist this part of the process. We want to just send out one email and get 100 people to sign up for our program. We want to launch our website and have ideal clients magically find us on Google. We want to skip the step of writing our book and just visualize ourselves opening up the *New York Times* and seeing it on the bestseller list. We want to avoid getting up at 5 a.m. every day to run or bike and just see ourselves strong and fast running down the street.

There are no skipping steps. You have to put in the work if you want to build a community of passionate ideal customers, not just a temporary group of people who are mesmerized by your sales letter, then leave you when they realize you only care about them when they give you money.

SLOW DOWN THE PACE OF CONNECTION

When my husband and I were courting almost two decades ago, he flew out to my home in Oakland, California. Short on time together the Sunday before he flew back to Phoenix on Monday, I planned an epic day for us. We started by driving to my hometown of San Anselmo for breakfast on San Anselmo Avenue, where I used to walk to school with my dad. After breakfast, we drove a few miles to Phoenix Lake and took a leisurely hike around the lake.

Our senses were heightened as we took in the beautiful redwood trees, rich earth, and abundant wildlife. I told him stories of riding my bike up to the lake as a little girl and spending hours reading a book in the branches of oak trees or chasing leaves in the stream with a stick. After our hike, we drove back across the bay to a powwow in Berkeley, where we walked around for a few hours, ate some lunch, and enjoyed the art, music, and dancing.

A man stopped us to greet Darryl and shake his hand. Then he gestured at me and asked Darryl, "What is the name of your temporary companion?" We laughed for hours afterward about that phrase. On the way home, we stopped to get some groceries. I made dinner and we ate by candlelight, looking out my big bay windows at the sparkling lights over Lake Merritt. Then we snuggled by the fire and shared a romantic evening.

To this day, we call it the longest and best day we ever had. It was relaxed, easy, and fun. We were fully present and felt alive. There was no pressure. We did things we enjoyed. It was, as I like to say, "easy breezy." Have you ever had a date like that?

Too much of modern marketing skips this step of relaxed, enjoyable getting to know you. When we know smart, supportive, connected people who can introduce us to ideal clients, recommend us for speaking engagements, and partner with us on exciting projects, our business flourishes. But in my experience both coaching people how to build a network as well as being on the receiving end of a lot of networking outreach, there is a big step that most people miss when consciously expanding their network: the Easy Breezy Zone.

I get at least three emails like this in my inbox every day:

Hi Pam!

I am a (type of service provider) that serves (this audience).

Can I pay you to write an article on (this topic—that very frequently has nothing to do with topics I write about) on your blog?

Sincerely,

Name of person I have never met.

Often, this comes from a company I can't identify because they don't put the name of the company under their signature. Nor do they include any sample articles.

Clearly, I am underwhelmed by this approach. Because it misses a huge part of what makes human connection really awesome: a normal, natural series of interactions that can, where there is common interest and chemistry, move into productive business relationships and opportunities.

THE EASY BREEZY ZONE

The Easy Breezy Zone considers that when you have *no relationship at all* with a new person, there are a number of ways you can reach out and make a connection that promotes respect and curiosity.

Ways like:

1. **Sending a love letter.** I love to send notes or emails that have no purpose other than to tell someone that I am absolutely in love with their work, listing the reasons why. The key is to write it from the heart and not ask for anything in return.

2. **Commenting on a blog or social media post.** I have met some of my dearest friends in the comment section of blogs or in conversation on social media. If you are interested in warming up a relationship with a new person, follow their work and engage with them in a thoughtful way. Most people will pay attention to who is taking part in a conversation on their site.

3. **Sharing a person's work on your social channels.** Because you are a true fan of the work of a person who you want to connect with, share their stuff when it is relevant to your audience. We all want our work to travel, and it shows that you value their perspective. I figure that the 1,000th time I mention John Legend in a speech, blog post, webinar, book, or tweet, he may start to take notice. (I am probably at time 899 so far!)

4. **Sharing time off the beaten path.** I love to get to know someone outside of a straight business context. When I was speaking at Jonathan and Stephanie Field's Good Life Camp a few years ago, I roped my then acquaintance Jeff Goins (whom you met in Chapter 2) into taking the train up with me from New York City. We ended up getting delayed and spent hours together sitting on benches in train stations, and even getting shushed for speaking too

loudly in a quiet car (in fairness, we didn't realize it was a quiet car). That trip allowed me to get to know Jeff in a whole new way, as we shared deep stories and deep laughter. Our friendship deepened, as did our connection with work. Now that travel is more unpredictable with global health crises and unstable weather, you can still set up some "off the beaten path" interactions with texts, instant messages, or Zoom catch-ups.

5. **Sending a useful article, handwritten card, or small gift.** Think of how you feel when your mom sends you a clipped newspaper article or a handwritten card. (As long as it isn't, "Why it is harder to get pregnant after forty and why you should start giving me grandkids now!") It is lovely to get a little note, quirky gift, or useful tidbit. You know that someone took time to prepare something and take it to the post office.

6. **Replying to an email newsletter.** It just takes a quick "hit reply" and a few comments to let your newsletter author know you appreciate their words. I have met many a new friend and colleague from some quick email exchange over a newsletter I wrote.

A Word of Caution

Use discernment in the Easy Breezy Zone the same way you would in a romantic courtship. Notice things like:

- Is there any natural personality chemistry?

- Does the person seem warm and open, or cold and standoffish?

- Does this activity feel genuine and nonpressured, or rushed and intense?

- Am I connecting with a real person or just the professional image I have of them?

- Am I watching for signs that there is mutual connection and respecting boundaries?

- Am I pretending to be in the Easy Breezy Zone, when really I am ready to pounce on a sale?

Make sure before you go straight for the transaction that you have spent some time investing in the Easy Breezy Zone.

CREATING YOUR SEEDING PLAN

The entire Widest Net Method hinges upon strategic and effective seeding. You can have the most powerful mission in the world, the clearest picture of your ideal client, the best offering in the marketplace, and a map of the best watering holes and partnerships to grow your audience. All that will mean nothing if you don't institute active seeding.

Seeding is what creates connection and momentum. Seeding is the consistent, methodical, and relational way you reach out to connect and share useful information, resources, and support to your ideal customers and partners. It should not feel like a tidal wave of activity, but rather like a slow, methodical drip, like 20 minutes of turning on your garden water to gently soak the ground.

A good indicator that you are a relational community builder, not a transactional one, is that after your position power or influence changes (due to leaving an organization, no longer having resources or political influence), people still want you to participate in conversations with them and build things together.

Relational community building centers on a true appreciation for the human you are connecting with, regardless of their perceived power or influence. These relationships tend to move slower, last longer, and go deeper.

Transactional community building centers being connected with people only when they can do something for you, and as soon as that power or influence goes away, the relationship is discarded. These relationships tend to start out hot and heavy, then end sharply and frigidly.

THE FOUR PHASES OF SEEDING

The Widest Net seeding method has four phases: survey your ecosystem map, seeding preparation, tiny marketing actions, and follow up.

Phase 1: Survey Your Ecosystem Map

All the work you have done in this book so far has prepared you for your seeding plan. From Chapters 1 to 5, you have created:

- Your business mission, and the bigger problem you are interested in contributing to solving with your work from Chapter 1.

- Your values, which serve as guideposts to the people you choose to work with, the culture you bring to life, and how you conduct yourself from Chapter 2.

- Your ideal customer profile, defined by a problem or aspiration from Chapter 3.

- Your customer journey, including all the steps in the journey that your customer needs to take from Chapter 4.

- Your starting list of watering holes and potential PB&J partners from Chapter 5.

With this information, you know why it is important to reach out, whom exactly you are reaching out to, and where you can find them. Use this data as a starting point for the next phase: preparation.

Phase 2: Seeding Preparation

Seeding preparation has two parts: philosophical and tactical.

Philosophical Preparation

It is really important to know that in early stage seeding conversations, the purpose of your online interactions or calls is not to close a sale. Sometimes, when the right mix of preparation and product fit come together, sales do happen, even on a first get-to-know-you call. But that is not the express purpose. The purpose of outreach in your Seeding Plan is to first show up as a warm and interested partner, with the primary goal of learning more about the world of your ideal customers. In our work at the K'é Main Street Learning Lab, we called this *Listen First.*

This philosophical orientation should quiet some of your fears of first connections, because you don't have to worry about launching into a big sales pitch. In my experience, a big sales pitch for first connections does not work, because it is not a natural first step in human connection. That is why it feels awkward and even assaulting to have a first-time commenter on your Facebook page pitch their services in their first comment. Or why it makes you want to immediately disconnect a LinkedIn contact when the first thing they do after connecting is send you a canned pitch in an instant message.

Humans need time to assess whether a business connection is ethical, competent and safe. Slow down.

Tactical Outreach Templates

If you, like Heather, are not naturally wired to know the kinds of questions and topics that are relevant and build engagement in early-stage conversations, it is very helpful to create some tactical templates that will help guide your conversations and ensure you don't freeze or fumble. These are not word-for-word scripts; they are just guides to make sure you show up in a way that is useful and not overbearing.

Heather and I worked on a very specific template to guide her get-to-know-you calls with ecosystem partners to avoid the awful situation she found herself in before. Here is an example of the template she used:

EXAMPLE OF "FIRST CONVERSATION" TEMPLATE FROM HEATHER KRAUSE'S OUTREACH:

Person's name (with pronunciation)

Express gratitude for connection

Purpose of the connection is to get to know you a bit more and understand what you are working on.

I wonder what we have in common?

Can you share a concrete example of a project you're working on?

Do you use data?

What is a specific example of data that you use?

What is one thing that frustrates you about the data you use in projects?

Is there anything I could do to support you in feeling happier about the equity you can achieve with data?

I work in data equity. We have developed the Data Equity Framework.

What would be a really useful tool for you?

Where do you hang out online?

Phase 3: Tiny Marketing Actions

To make your specific Seeding Plan feasible and sustainable, you need to break your tasks down into tiny marketing actions (TMAs).

I define TMAs as:

> **Small daily marketing actions, delivered consistently over a long period of time, to build your brand, your business, and your bank account.**

These actions can be things like:

- Sending an email to check in with a past client.

- Creating a fun image on Canva and sharing it on Instagram or Facebook.

- Reaching out to a reporter at a publication that serves your audience and offering yourself as an expert resource.

- Responding to a question on a Facebook thread, demonstrating your expertise.

- Sending a card to a favorite peer or colleague who is likely to be a good referral source.

The key to developing a habit of TMAs is to organize your efforts so when you have a 5- or 10-minute break in your day, you can seed a few TMAs. (For a Tiny Marketing Action Playbook, visit https://pamelaslim.com/tma-playbook/.)

Phase 4: Seeding Follow-Up

The nature of TMAs is that you will likely hear back from only a small percentage of people you reach out to. Some will be too busy. Others may not be interested and simply ignore you.

But there will be people who will be excited to hear from you and say things like:

> "It is so great to hear from you! I love what you are working on, do you have any information about it I can share with my team?"

> "I would love to set up a time to talk with you, do you have an online scheduler?"

> "Your graphic design sounds amazing, do you have a portfolio of your work?"

> "Who have you worked with before?"

You should prepare for positive and interested reactions by creating and organizing the following:

- Materials that describe your products and services, like a PDF or web page.

- A link to your online scheduler, or if you have high volume, a connection with the assistant that manages your calendar.

- Samples of your work, where appropriate.

- Lists of publicly shareable clients.

If you do not yet have these materials in place, don't let that stop you from doing your TMAs. A great way to motivate you to get this follow-up material designed is to have an interested potential customer ask you for it.

100 CONVERSATIONS

Where Heather Krause initially loathed the idea of reaching out to unknown connections, the Adaway Group CEO Desiree Adaway was wired for it. A natural extrovert with a lifetime of work organizing diverse communities, first as a camp director, then in corporate, then as director of Global Volunteer Mobilization for Habitat for Humanity, where she oversaw 1,000,000 volunteers worldwide annually, Desiree loves talking to people.

While teaching a mastermind program, she had marketing expert Shenee Howard as a guest speaker. Shenee suggested that Desiree's mastermind participants talk with 100 strangers to expand their awareness, connections, and audience. Desiree loved the idea as a way to model learning from her community and becoming more comfortable with difficult conversations.

She jumped on it right away. She set up a simple scheduling link for a 30-minute meeting. Then she shared it on social media with the following parameters:

1. This connection must be the first time we have met (we are strangers).

2. This conversation is completely private. I will not record it, keep notes, or share any stories.

3. I will never tell anyone we had this conversation (she literally told them "It is like I am your waxer. Unless you acknowledge you know me in public, I will never acknowledge I know you.")

4. There are fewer than five questions.

The first set of questions for her 100 conversations were:

1. What do you love?

2. What do you do?

3. What made you talk to a stranger?

After more and more of her work turned toward diversity, equity, and inclusion, and after more and more public outrage and conversation over people in her Black community being killed by the police, she shifted her questions to specifically focus on race. Her questions became:

1. Who are you?

2. What identities do you use to navigate the world?

3. What did your parents teach you about race?

4. What was the first time you either heard or said a racial slur?

Desiree conducted these totally confidential conversations for years, talking to over 800 strangers. She said it was a deeply moving and informative practice, and it became apparent to her how many folks from all backgrounds were afraid to talk about race. Many harbored deep pain, shame, or guilt, sometimes over things that had happened decades ago. While she kept her word to not record, track, or share any of the conversations, she did notice themes in the conversations that informed her public work.

In addition to her conversations with strangers, Desiree also did a number of other regular seeding activities on Facebook, like:

- Always saying happy birthday to every single one her Facebook friends.

- Writing daily inspirational posts (most no more than two sentences).

- Posing challenging questions on Facebook and asking folks to respond in a private message, rather than a comment.

This deep connection with community has had a big impact on her business. After six years of doing these quiet seeding activities, her public classes and webinars (often cotaught with colleagues Ericka Hines and Jessica Fish) went from having scores of people attending to hundreds, then thousands. It helped her create a niche around racial equity, not general DEI (diversity, equity, and inclusion) work. And it deeply informed how identity and socialization played into the work.

Desiree and her team at the Adaway Group (https://adawaygroup.com) now do large engagements with companies like Google, Intuit, Facebook, United Airlines, Adobe, Fast Company, Inc., Girl Scouts, American Jewish World Service, and more. Regular seeding activities have transformed Desiree's business, and now her work is helping transform the world.

THE SPROUTING EFFECT

At K'é Main Street Learning Lab, our Seeding Plan brought forth what we came to describe as the Sprouting Effect. After we spent a lot of time in Listen First mode and built relationships with leaders, they would approach us about holding an event in the space. Once we were certain it was a fit with our mission, they would run the first test pilot. If they liked it and wanted to continue, their event would become part of the ongoing schedule at the Lab.

What we began to notice is that the main source of new leaders approaching us to host events was attendees at events hosted by others.

Isha Cogborn's Startup Life Support sprouted La'Vista Jones's Boss Talk series.

The Phoenix Indian Center's Navajo language classes sprouted a Native book club circle led by Bobbi Nez.

The Freelancer's Union meeting sprouted Ita Udo-Ema's YouTube Creator's Academy.

The Modern Spirit gathering of traditional healers and wellness consultants sprouted Joey Bellus's Meditation classes, and later the opening of his own personal training and personal growth facility, Optimum Performance Training or OPT.

Downtown Mesa Association's board meeting sprouted strategic planning for the Mesa City Council.

Mesa Arts Center's Creative Catalyst local artist gallery s how conversations sprouted *The Collective*, a leadership program teaching leadership through the arts.

Jen Duff's Mesa City Council campaign kickoff sprouted Davina Lyons's Tribe Authentic Woman bimonthly workshops.

Morning Star Leadership for Native youth sprouted to the filming of REZponse YouTube series by Indigenous CC founders Melody Lewis and Turquoise Devereaux.

It got to the point when during the presidential election for the Navajo Nation, the campaigns for both candidates, Joe Shirley and Jonathan Nez, reached out to us to host meet and greets for registered Navajo voters living in the Phoenix metropolitan area. "We heard you were a hub for Navajos in the valley," they said. My husband and I looked at each other and said, "I guess this is working!"

You will also experience the Sprouting Effect when your happy customers start to refer their friends and colleagues to you. Because your audience and profile are growing, partners might reach out to you to collaborate, as opposed to you having to reach out to them. An event planner may see you speak at a conference, then ask you to speak at their conference in the future.

Seeds sprout, and it will translate into momentum in your business.

PREPARE FOR HEARTBREAK

Thus far, I have been extolling the virtues of building real, human relationships and not looking at people like numbers in your business.

To be responsible, I need to also tell you that operating from a relational perspective will sometimes be extremely difficult. I think of one of my favorite lines from my favorite movie of all time, *Moonstruck*, when Nicolas Cage's character says to Cher's character: "The snowflakes are perfect. The stars are perfect. Not us. Not us! We are here to ruin ourselves and to break our hearts and love the wrong people and 'die.'"

- When you have meaningful relationships with your customers, and you care about how they feel about you, it will be hard to hear feedback that they are unhappy with something in your business.

- When you mess up in public and say something offensive (we all do and will), you will have to face the heat of people you know, and don't know, who are mad at you.

- When you transition to a new business model, you may need to stop serving some of your favorite customers. This will hurt. A lot.

- You may enter into a partnership with good intentions, and through experience, find you are not the best fit. This can feel awkward and scary.

- A beloved customer or client may choose to stop working with you and go work with someone you may not like or is not as talented as you are, and you may get jealous.

There is no way around this. You will survive this heartbreak by remembering three things:

1. It is your job to serve the mission of your business. If you have chosen a mission that has deep meaning to you, the discomfort is worth it.

2. Don't take things personally. This second agreement from Don Miguel Ruiz's powerful book, *The Four Agreements*, will save you a lot of heartache. Even though it may feel like it, you are not your business.

3. The heartbreak of real human relationships is better than the heartlessness of a transactional business. It does not build character or create meaning to dehumanize your customers.

I summarized my community-building ethos into a manifesto.

COMMUNITY BUILDER'S MANIFESTO

Many of us spend time in our neighborhoods, businesses, social, and spiritual spaces working to bring awesome people together.

Who doesn't want a bustling, downtown, a packed event, or a thriving online forum?

We call this work "community building."

But what does community building actually mean? How does it behave? How is it structured?

Based especially on my work the last five years building the Main Street Learning Lab at K'é and three decades of gathering people in business, in the arts, and online, this is how I choose to define community building.

Community is the earth, water, air, and sunshine for our sense of belonging and purpose.
It is the ecosystem—the set of people, places, structures, organizations, resources, and behaviors—that allow us to feel like we are seen, heard, understood, and valued, and where we find the tools to reach our goals.

Our best work takes place in a community that we understand and that understands us. That is why it is natural and prudent to build your business or career with people who "get you."

At different times in our life, we need different types of community. That is why we can spend time in a place, organization, or group of friends feeling like we totally belong until, one day, we don't.

As we change, our need for community changes, which is why many are fluid, appearing and disappearing after they have lived out their purpose.

You never build community by riding into town on a horse with a bullhorn.

You discover community by sitting quietly on a bench in the shade in a town square (literal or metaphorical), observing the way people interact with each other and listening intently to the person who sits down next to you.

If you perceive there is no community, you are usually wrong. Our fundamental yearning is to connect with each other, so sometimes these meeting places and relationships are hidden, tucked away in corners.

Magic community building questions are: "Who is here? Who is not here? Why aren't they here?" If you really dig into these questions in your own neighborhoods, online spaces, places of worship, workplaces, organizations, and community events, you will uncover a wealth of useful data.

And don't stop at your first answer to *"Why aren't they here?"* Keep asking. Challenge your thinking. Engage with people who are not in your community and ask them that question. "Well, I asked once, but they didn't come so I guess they are not interested" is not a valid response.

Support first, then build.

A common inclination is to think the answer to building community is to create new events or forums. We assume that people haven't been gathering because the existing events are inadequate.

That may be true. It may also not be true.

Before building anything new, go to existing event organizers and ask, "What do you need to strengthen what you are doing?"

Sometimes it is marketing help. Or resources. Or space. Or new ideas. Or encouragement.

If your first answer is always to build something new, you may be inadvertently draining huge emotional, financial, and physical labor from people in the community who have been working to build their own events for years or even decades.

To build new relationships, demonstrate your commitment to the community by first supporting what is already there. Then you can decide together what else might be needed to fill the gaps.

We connect around shared purpose, but bond over witnessing the truth of our lived experience.
Community doesn't replace sociology and history.

Many strive to create magical spaces where we are only connected by the things that we have in common, which can be many.

But it is not inclusive or loving to deny the history of our own experiences. It is not inclusive or loving to refuse to acknowledge that we are treated very differently as we walk or wheel down the sidewalk on the way to shared spaces, based on how we appear, who we love, or where we worship (if at all). Denying these differences shears our connection, it does not enhance it.

Learning about each other's lived experience can give us new ways to think about when, where, how, and why we meet.

Our health, safety, and well-being are related to our understanding of and care for our differences.

We speak truth and honor boundaries.
I do not like conflict. And I have learned to embrace it, since it is impossible to do anything meaningful without making mistakes, running into differing opinions, or pissing someone off.

It is important that we speak clearly, openly, and honestly to each other when we don't agree on something.

It is important that we listen with an open heart and curiosity.

It is important to be flexible in thinking and open to change, or as my friend Bob Sutton likes to phrase it, "Strong opinions, weakly held."

It is important that we say no when we need to.

It is important that we respect hearing no when we want to hear yes.

It is impossible to build healthy community structures with unhealthy behaviors and lack of boundaries.

Resentment festers. Unsaid words turn into unfortunate outbursts. Weak boundaries turn into depleted bodies, tired minds, and weary spirits.

We don't all have to be friends. Or like the same things.
My best friend of 37 years has never seen a *Star Wars* movie. She is lukewarm on John Legend. She doesn't feel the need to take pictures of her newly painted toes. I am passionate about every one of these things.

We have a lot of friends in common, and we also have friends who will probably never connect.

What we share is connection to purpose, and to the health, safety, well-being, and joy of each other.

We can be in community and not be good friends.

We can be good friends, and not share every community.

Enduring community is built around a mission, not a person.

By definition, community and ecosystems are made up of many different people, parts, and systems.

When you are interested in building community, you may take on the roles of convener, encourager, or spokesperson.

But if you start to notice that without you convening, encouraging, or speaking, that nothing happens—you are building an empire, not a community.

Define together what you are working on. What are your goals? What is the vision? Who is it for? How will you know if you have reached it?

Spread leadership around. If everything will fall apart without you holding it together, let it fall apart. A new, more sustainable structure will appear from the rubble.

Any significant cultural, legal, economic, social or innovative change comes from a large collective of leaders working on it.

Community building is capacity building.
In community, it is our job to help each other be better, stronger, more capable, competent, and secure.

Our engagement with each other is an endless journey of personal transformation and skill building.

We want to end our days together feeling more alive, empowered, and bold.

Our one daily commitment is to never let an opportunity pass to show how much we care for each other, how much we believe in each other and how much we are committed to growth and change in each other. With this mindset, amazing things can happen.

In whatever way you work to make your home, neighborhood, workplace, business, or organization a more welcoming, vibrant, fun, and effective community, thank you.

We are stronger together.

EXERCISE: Seeding Plan

Timeframe (check one):	• Month • Quarter • Year
Survey the Ecosystem:	Evaluate the Ecosystem Worksheet from Chapter 5, Who are the best seeding partners to start? • List watering holes: • List potential PB&J partners for get-to-know-you conversations: • List events you would like to speak at: • List media hubs you want to approach:
Preparation Checklist:	What do I need to prepare in order to take TMAs? • Email outreach templates • About page on website updated • PDFs or program overviews • Scheduling links
Seeding Outreach: TMAs	What pace and frequency will I do my TMAs? How will I track them?
Watering and Cultivation	What is my follow-up plan for my TMAs?

SEEDING PAYS OFF

By early 2021, Heather's We All Count initiative was taking off. She was conducting training for major foundations, respected universities, and thousands of individuals inside the data science sector. Her business was generating impressive financial results, allowing her to expand her team and invest in marketing support. Most important, the work itself was changing the outcomes for her clients. Heather taught me that everyone can learn to seed, when believing in an important enough mission.

Or as she would tell you, "If I can do it, I guarantee that you can do it!"

STEP SEVEN:
THE BEACON YOU LIGHT

Let your watchword be order
and your beacon beauty.
—Daniel Burnham

Debbie Reber and her husband, Darron, spent years figuring out how to best support their son in school and in life. Asher, their neurodivergent son (profoundly gifted, ADHD, sensory processing challenges, and more) struggled to find the right school fit. "We felt like failures when it came to managing meltdowns or dealing with difficult behavior. We were pretty sure we were being judged by other parents, teachers, and family." Not sure if things were hard because they were bad at parenting or if there was something going on with their son, they didn't know where to start, where to turn, and who to seek support from.

Debbie found that many of the websites or organizations that she researched didn't speak to her, nor did they help her figure out a plan for her son while supporting herself in the process. Her best leads came from word-of-mouth from other parents who had been down the road before her. She said, "Figuring out what to do and where to turn next was like geocaching without a GPS."

Debbie decided to start a website and build a movement so that other parents of neurodivergent, or what she calls "differently wired" children, could move forward with what their kids needed in a way that felt positive and hopeful for the whole family. It was a big market, especially considering at least 20 percent of children are neurodivergent,[1] or differently wired, like her son.

It was at this point that she reached out to start working together and Tilt Parenting was formed.

CHOOSING A BEACON

Debbie was very deliberate in her approach to building Tilt Parenting. A writer and coach by trade, she had already written numerous books, and had experience in documentary and television production. She could have chosen a whole range of different ways to package the content for this movement. For Tilt Parenting, she decided to choose a podcast as the main vehicle for audience building and to share her point of view. She said:

I have been a podcast consumer for ages, so once I started developing the Tilt Parenting "revolution," I knew the primary content vehicle would be a podcast for parents. It felt like an ideal medium for many reasons. For one, parents of differently wired children have so little time to devote to their own learning—I wanted to give them access to experts where they could listen on their own time, consume a 30- or 40-minute interview, and leave with at least one nugget or aha moment that could help their family work better.

I also love that there is no limit to the episodes, topics, and guests I can feature—there are always more experts, authors, perspectives, and neurodivergent changemakers to bring onto the show. Last, producing a podcast taps into my personal value of personal growth and being a lifelong learner . . . I just want to keep learning about all the things and sharing them with others who would benefit.

For six chapters, I have cautioned you against barreling into a room on your white horse shouting about your services, instead recommending that you spend time listening to and learning about your customers' issues, challenges, and aspirations.

I have railed against building a singular empire and pretending that you have all the answers to your customer's problems. I have been sharing the multiple ways in which your market will explode as you center your ideal customer's journey and connect to multiple watering holes in your customer's ecosystem

through guest appearances, joint promotions, and partnerships. Now it is time for you to set up your own, bright, shiny,
unique spotlight that tells your ideal customers, peers, and
partners:

This is who I am.

This is what I believe.

This is my theory of change.

This is my point of view.

Here are my solutions to your problems.

I call this bright, shining light your *Beacon*.

WHAT KINDS OF BEACONS ARE THERE?

There are two kinds of Beacons: Pop-up and Permanent.

Pop-up Beacons could be:

- A special event

- A well-curated dinner party

- A onetime video or writing product that is not tied
  to a longer series

- A limited time speaking or workshop tour

- A limited scope webinar series

Permanent Beacons are things like:

- Email newsletter

- Podcast or radio show

- Blog

- Primary social media satellites (Facebook, Twitter, LinkedIn, Pinterest, YouTube, TikTok, or other)

- A brick-and-mortar location

- An ongoing meetup

- An annual conference

Note that for in-person Beacons like a brick-and-mortar space, a meetup, or a conference, you also need to have a primary content Beacon to attract an audience to the space.

THE PURPOSE OF A BEACON

Your Beacon is the primary, but not the only, place where you share your point of view and centralize your body of work. It should answer the question your ideal customers ask you: "Where is the best place for me to get to know you and your work?" From this Beacon, each time you produce new content, you can amplify the message by publicizing it on other social media satellites, listed earlier. For example, if your Beacon is a podcast, part of the process of publishing each episode could include creating small graphics about the episode on Canva to post on LinkedIn, Twitter, and Facebook, then including a blurb about your new episode in your email newsletter.

Choosing your primary Beacon requires some analysis. Here are some factors to consider:

- What is your communication strength? (Writing? Audio? Video?)

- What are your goals with this Beacon?

- What is the preferred communication vehicle for your ideal customer? (Where are they already hanging out or consuming content?)

- What do you own (in terms of digital real estate)? (If your Beacon is on a social media satellite, you can get kicked off and lose access to your audience.)

- What is the technology involved in producing content for this Beacon?

- What are the costs involved in the production of content on this Beacon?

- What Beacon are you likely to be most consistent with?

WHAT MAKES A GREAT BEACON?

It is not enough to select a central place to share your content and body of work. If you want to get traction and attract an audience, it needs to include the following elements:

- **A clear and distinct point of view amid a smart ecosystem.** Your choice of beacon should showcase your unique take on solving the core problem that drives your mission. It addresses:

  - ▸ What is missing from the conversation?
  - ▸ Whose important perspective is not being shared?
  - ▸ What obvious truths are being ignored?
  - ▸ What critical steps are not being covered?

- **A compelling voice.** The voice of your Beacon should be authentic and clear. Your audience needs to make an emotional connection with you or the people on your team who are producing content for the Beacon. For that to happen, you have to tap an internal place of communication that allows your real voice to come out. This includes humor, depth, truth, emotion, and perspective.

- **Well-produced content.** There is a lot of content out there on the Internet. To keep your community interested in coming back, you have to pay attention to the production quality of your content, or in the case of a physical space, your events. At a minimum, production quality doesn't interfere with the audience experience. At a premium, the production quality enhances the audience experience.

- **Consistent cadence.** Establishing a consistent cadence is a key part of developing a relationship with your ideal customers. When your content is useful and well-produced, they will look forward to it and tell their friends about it. Choose a realistic publishing schedule and stick to it (caveat—do not get so hung up in perfect cadence that you don't produce).

- **Adaptive and relevant.** Not only will your audience get tired of the same themes or topics, but you will also. Adjust and adapt content to what is happening for your audience and in the world at large.

- **Shows a depth of your body of work.** Your Beacon is a place where you can go deep on topics that are important and relevant to you. You can produce longer articles or white papers in your newsletter or produce an interesting series on your podcast or YouTube channel.

- **In aggregate, helps your audience solve their core problem.** As you pull these writings, episodes, or events together, they form a useful catalog of content that can become books or content series or training programs. In aggregate, they help your ideal customers receive your complete solution to their core problem.

- **Curation.** Producing your own content is not the only way to create content for your Beacon. Your skill at curating content from others around the core problem you solve can be extremely valuable to your audience. This can also save time and headache if content creation is not your joy or strength.

BEACON EXAMPLES

There are so many great examples of well-constructed Beacons. Here are a few of my favorites:

Email Newsletters

James Clear's 3-2-1 Newsletter

https://jamesclear.com/newsletter

James Clear, bestselling author of *Atomic Habits*, has a very distinct and clean format to his newsletter, which he sends out once a week to over 1,000,000 subscribers. His normal posts include three ideas, two quotes, and one question.

Ann Handley's Total Annarchy

https://annhandley.com/newsletter

Ann Handley, author and founder of MarketingProfs, shares insight, examples, and humor when writing about "things I am doing and things worth sharing."

Morning Brew

https://www.morningbrew.com/daily

Morning Brew is my favorite daily news aggregator newsletter. Their writing is sharp and witty, and they employ lots of genius ways to engage their readers, like having a five-question quiz at the end of every week that tests their readers on content shared in the daily newsletter. They also have lots of spin-off newsletters like Marketing Brew, Retail Brew, Emerging Tech Brew, and podcasts Business Casual and Founder's Journey.

Tamsen Webster's Red Thread Newsletter

https://tamsenwebster.com/newsletter/

Tamsen demonstrates a rich and deliberate approach to teaching about her core methodology, the Red Thread, which is also the name of her book. She dives in deep to core ideas, using real client examples. You not only walk away from reading her newsletter learning new insights, but you often get access to useful tools, templates, and formulas that teach you how to be a more effective communicator.

Rohit Bhargava's Non-Obvious Newsletter

https://www.nonobvious.com/

Rohit is an author and speaker who writes about business trends. The mission of his newsletter is "to help leaders, organizations and curious minds learn the habits that allow them to see what others miss and win the future." As a reader, I look forward to strange and interesting stories ranging from "pajama shaming" to "NASA publishes space ethics."

Social Media Satellites

There are a lot of amazing creators out there, and more social media satellites than would be practical to list in a book. Here is a sampling of some of my favorites:

Facebook

Humans of New York

https://www.facebook.com/humansofnewyork

Brandon Stanton started Humans of New York as a photography project, with the aim of taking 10,000 pictures of New Yorkers. He started to interview his subjects, in addition to filming them. His moving stories led to thousands of comments and shares. Now with over 20 million followers and multiple books, it is a textbook example of how to do Social Media Beacons right.

Healthy Active Natives

https://www.facebook.com/groups/Healthyactivenatives

Waylon Pee Pahona started this Facebook group to inspire his fellow Native American relatives to get healthy and active. Now 75,000 Native American members strong, it provides a constant source of support and inspiration for members that span North America.

Twitter

Small Biz Lady

https://twitter.com/smallbizlady

Melinda Emerson, aka Small Biz Lady, has almost 300,000 Twitter followers and uses this Beacon to host Twitter chats, share business tips, and alert her followers about her multiple events and offerings.

Small Business Trends

https://twitter.com/SmallBizTrends

Anita Campbell curates Small Business Trends and brings small business owners and the companies that serve them the news, advice, and resources they need.

Instagram

Color Me Magic (for the Disney lovers out there)

https://www.instagram.com/colormemagic/

Demonstrating fun, whimsy, and made-for-Instagram beautiful color photos, Color Me Magic showcases pop culture, especially Disney Princesses, styled by founder Courtney Quinn. Her photos lead to a store where you can buy a wide variety of brightly colored fashion and merchandise.

Chipotle

https://www.instagram.com/chipotle/

Chipotle mixes its own content with user-generated content, all with wit and humor. It shows that bigger brands can still have fun with an authentic voice, while celebrating the passion its customers have for its food.

Brick and Mortar Beacons

K'é Main Street Learning Lab, Mesa, Arizona

https://pamelaslim.com/ke

Our K'é Main Street Learning Lab plays a very deliberate role by being situated right in the middle of Main Street, providing a welcome gathering spot for over 5,000 community members over the past five years. It is a flexible and colorful space, filled with art and a gigantic white board wall that has been the canvas for hundreds of business plans, community initiatives, and conversations.

Angelica Perez-Litwin's Lumin Center

http://www.lumincenter.com/

Angelica Perez is a long-time therapist from New York who has built a body of work to address every angle surrounding issues of mental health for her Latinx patients, including founding a thriving Facebook group Latinas Think Big.

After moving to Greenville, South Carolina, with her family, she opened a beautiful brick-and-mortar space called Lumin Center. It offers what she calls "Modern Therapy," which includes mental and emotional resilience, couple's therapy, career mentoring, school admissions mentoring, and self-care mentoring. Lumin Center also hosts virtual therapy featuring therapists from diverse mental health specialty areas, but also from different cultural backgrounds to address the unique challenges faced by their patients.

Therapy is delivered in a variety of ways, in person in the office, in virtual sessions, and even via email.

SOCIAL MEDIA FACEBOOK GROUP BEACON CASE STUDY

Facebook Groups are extremely popular Beacons for many business owners who want to start to build community and connect with ideal customers.

Lamar Tyler and Ronnie Tyler, cofounders of Black and Married with Kids and Traffic Sales and Profit, have created an extremely impressive community online. The mission of their overall brand is to "Uplift, encourage and support the African American community." Starting with the Black and Married with Kids blog in 2007, they went on to produce seven full-length films and 12 books, hold workshops and conferences, and even hosted cruises. They have had media appearances on CNN, HLN, the *Today Show*, and more. They have over 600,000 followers on social media and have served over 51,000 customers in 50 states and in just about every country in the world.

After achieving a lot of success with their first brand, Lamar was fielding all kinds of questions about techniques he had used to grow the Black and Married with Kids business. He and Ronnie started Traffic Sales and Profit as a way to help African American entrepreneurs scale to six, seven figures and beyond, using the tools and techniques of online marketing.

A core part of the strategy for Traffic Sales and Profit is using Facebook groups as a Beacon to provide a safe and empowering space for their Black members. Lamar says:

You can find information about business in so many groups around the internet. But there is this last 10 to 15 percent of content that is cultural for our community based on our lived experience. Knowing we are safe to share stories, worship, and have a cultural connection is very important to our members. Self-love doesn't mean we hate everyone else.

In this 25,000 member Facebook group, a free entryway is provided to do deeper work with Traffic Sales and Profit's paid events, coaching, courses, and masterminds. In addition, a generous community answers questions, shares resources, provides support, and celebrates wins. Lamar says "We don't have to do a lot of moderating because the kinds of people who are attracted to our community have a heart for service. They create a culture of caring for and taking care of each other."

In their last 2020 mastermind cohort, they had 40 six-figure and 15 seven-figure business owners. The volume of members and stellar reputation of their brand attracts a lot of attention from companies wanting to partner with them. Having done big sponsor partnerships in the past with companies like General Mills, Lamar and Ronnie said, "Given the relationship we have with our community, we have a lot of influence. So we are discerning about who we partner with."

When asked what qualities they look for in outside partners, Lamar listed the following qualities:

- Do they have a great customer journey?

- What is their path and purpose? For SaaS companies— what is their future?

- Do they stand up and do what they say they are going to do?

- Do they have a good track record for people who have used their products or services?

- Do they treat each member of our community as well as they treat us as owners?

- Do they have diverse teams and staff at all levels of their team and company?

"It is not about being perfect," Lamar said. "We want to work with people who truly care about our community. We want people who will be honest, and not just say what they think they should say."

Moving forward, Lamar and Ronnie are building and investing in their community. They just acquired and renovated a physical space that will be their company headquarters in Atlanta where they can host events and workshops. Their work centers around three pillars:

1. **Community giveback.** This is for nonprofits that are traditionally underfunded. They have already raised over $80,000 for these projects.

2. **Youth initiative.** They will provide scholarships to events so young entrepreneurs can be inspired by the great entrepreneurs in their programs and on stage at their events.

3. **Investment.** With a history of systemic predatory lending in the Black community, they will focus on providing loans and investments to help their members grow and scale their businesses.

GREAT BEACONS HAVE STRONG MANIFESTOS

When I first started working with Debbie Reber, she came with an extremely well-written vision for Tilt Parenting, which was the Tilt Parenting Manifesto she had developed in a class taught by Jonathan Fields. This manifesto outlined four critical things that guided the development of her Beacon:

- TiLT founder Debbie Reber's personal story in shifting her experience raising her twice-exceptional son. She moved from frustration, stress, and isolation to true acceptance, optimism, and possibility.

- Why the current parenting paradigm is broken and outdated, especially for parents with atypical kids.

- While our journey raising our differently wired children is unique to us and who our children are, we are tied together through shared experiences of parenting outside the lines.

- The 10 things parents everywhere can start doing right now to take a lead in shifting the parenting paradigm to one that embraces both our children and our experience in raising them.

With this very compelling and well-organized manifesto, creating content for her podcast Beacon was extremely straightforward, because there was a very clear point of view. To read and download the Tilt Parenting Manifesto, go here: https://tiltparenting.com/recommended-resources/manifesto/.

BEING AUTHENTIC ONLINE

My favorite question when I was teaching a marketing class many years ago was "How do I appear to be authentic online?" My answer was a bit cheeky, but true: "The best way to appear authentic online is to actually *be* authentic online."

I always advocate for being transparent about who you are, what you believe, and how you truly behave, in front of or behind the curtain. It is fine to talk about politics, important and sensitive social topics, or parts of your personal journey that are key to your identity as a person and leader.

This does not mean that you have to share all your personal information or spill messy details of your relationships on your social media. You want to use discernment. I have a few examples of things you might not want to share through your Beacons:

- **A speaker gets off stage and tweets "I crushed that talk! We converted 80% of the audience!"** Why were you there on stage, from the audience's perspective? Was it to "convert them to your offer" or to offer useful, thought-provoking information and ideas to help them solve their problems? When your message focuses only on your own financial results, and not the results obtained by your clients, this tells your community, "You are here to help me get rich." That is not very inspirational.

- **"I fired that a*hole customer who was driving me crazy. Good riddance!"** When you use vague and harsh terms on social media, your customers may think you are talking about them, even if you aren't. Maybe there were two recent scenarios, one where you peacefully gave a refund and stopped working with someone, and another that was more contentious where you ended on poor terms. How are your clients to know who you are talking about? And more important, why would you ever want to broadcast that you think that any client, current or past, is an a*hole?

- **"My man left, my dog ran away, and my truck broke down. I have no idea how I am going to deliver my work to my clients this week**." We have all been there. Or we have listened to that country song! There have been many times throughout my 25 years in business when I have thought, "If people could see the mess I am in now, they would never believe it!" Times like these are really awful,

but they are part of the human journey. There is nothing wrong with you if a bunch of difficult things happen
in your life. This is when you need to call your mom or
dad, bawl your eyes out, have coffee with your best friend,
and come up with a good plan. It is probably not the best
time to let it all out online. My friend Mark Silver wrote a
blog post a few years ago about "The Car Wreck of Being
Authentic," and the importance of discerning *when* you
are ready to share your personal difficulties with your
community. He says:

> *No, I don't have to show up as perfect. But I want*
> *anything I share to be expressed consciously in ser-*
> *vice to others, and not as an emotional/situational*
> *vomiting up of a mess. You shouldn't have to clean*
> *up after me, I have a support system who can help*
> *me with that. And then I can tell you how I got*
> *through the mess.*

Discerning what to share, when, and with whom is a key
part of business mastery. It is not easy, and there are no hard and
fast rules, since each business owner and audience are different.
Here are some suggestions for determining when to hit publish:

Why am I sharing this message? Is this to make you feel
better or to provide value to your audience?

**Does the spirit of this message reflect and harmonize
with the spirit of my brand?** Note that "harmonize"
does not mean that you never address any tough issues
or share strong personal views on social issues—it just

means that the views are in harmony with the purpose and vision of your business.

Am I sharing this to incite thoughtful discussion or inspiration in my community or to get a quick rush of personal positive reinforcement? No judgment here— we have all done it! Who doesn't like a huge rush of likes on social media?

Is this an important part of the story of my body of work? Will this contribute to an ongoing narrative and conversation about the work you care about? Does it include the stories of the customers you work with? Does it provide insight or tools that solve the problems you care about with your business?

Deciding exactly what to share on your Beacon can be hard to discern. It is not about being perfect, it is about being intentional.

BRICK-AND-MORTAR BEACON CASE STUDY AND PLANNING TOOL: ASU INNOVATION STUDIO

In my little downtown area of Mesa, Arizona, a big Beacon project is emerging. Arizona State University is building a downtown campus just two blocks from our K'é Main Street Learning Lab. An old city library building is being refurbished into an Innovation Studio, owned by our city government, but run by the ASU Entrepreneurship and Innovation department/ division. Downtown Mesa is designing an Innovation District, a concept developed by the Brookings Institute.

On the surface, it is great for the community to have access to a free public building as well as to have access to programming from ASU, named the Top University for Innovation five years in a row from *U.S. News and World Report.* But as ASU was gathering community input for programming ideas, it became clear that they needed to approach this Beacon design with a deep understanding of the ecosystem of spaces in the local area. There are already scores of physical spaces in the few square blocks of the downtown Mesa area where Innovation Studio is located that produce, or will produce, events for the entrepreneurial community. Spaces like:

Our own K'é Main Street Learning Lab

Visit Mesa (the Visitor's Bureau)

The East Valley Hispanic Chamber of Commerce

The Mesa Chamber of Commerce

Heatsync Labs (a maker space)

Coworking spaces under construction, due to open in the next 12 to 18 months

Mesa Arts Center (a large regional art center with all kinds of beautiful meeting space)

Mesa Artspace Lofts (a residential community for artists, with community gallery space)

Local churches

Other governmental buildings

East Valley Institute of Technology

Benedictine University

Cafes and restaurants with meeting spaces

Paid event space

And more new spaces opening every month

What if the programming at the Innovation Studio inadvertently took people and resources away from the other organizations?

The success of a physical, brick-and-mortar Beacon is based on its unique place within the ecosystem. What can you provide that will be highly complementary and unique to what is already there?

Approach

Working together with community partners, ASU is going through a specific Beacon mapping process that includes:

- Assessing what is already there through scores of interviews and mapping

- Identifying the unique strengths of the Innovation Studio

- Clarifying their audience

- Clarifying goals

- Creating a programming map

- Creating an ongoing communication plan

In support of ASU's downtown partnership, I developed this Physical Space Beacon Framework, which we will use to support programming decisions for the new space.

Goal of Innovation District

This is a general description of an Innovation District from the Brookings Institute, but a more precise definition will be created for the Downtown Mesa Innovation District through Beacon Conversations.

Facilitate the creation and commercialization of new ideas and support metropolitan economies by growing jobs in ways that leverage their distinct economic attributes. These districts build on and revalue the intrinsic qualities of cities: proximity, density, authenticity, and vibrant places. Given the proximity of many districts to low-income neighborhoods and the large number of subbaccalaureate jobs many provide, their intentional development can be a tool to help connect disadvantaged populations to employment and educational opportunities.[2]

Stakeholders in Innovation District

Who are the stakeholders in the Innovation District? Who are the partners and primary beneficiaries?

Stakeholder	Organization or Areas	Role

Primary Beneficiaries	Organization or Neighborhood	Role

Ecosystem Partners

Who else in the geographic area is working toward the goal of the Innovation District, who are they serving, and what is their core purpose?

Name of Organization	Location	Audience	Core Purpose

Core Purpose: Innovation Studio

What gaps exist in the spaces and organizations that drive the core purpose of the Innovation Studio? In other words, what unique value and contribution can the Innovation Studio bring?

Stakeholders of the Innovation Studio

- Who is driving (curating) the programmatic design of the studio? (What does ASU do versus others?)

- Who is accountable for the decisions of the studio?

- What is the decision-making process for the development and growth of the studio?

- Who is impacted by the decisions of the studio?

Core Activities

- What kinds of activities, programs, or events take place at this location?

- What kinds of activities, programs, or events are not a fit for this location?

Communication

- What communication vehicles are needed to ensure all stakeholders are informed, engaged, and excited about the space?

- Which unique communication vehicles need to be used for particular stakeholders?

  Examples:
  - ▶ Newsletter
  - ▶ Social channels (Facebook, Instagram, LinkedIn, Snapchat, TikTok, YouTube)

> ► Web portal
> ► Flyers
> ► In-person or web meetings
> ► Podcast
> ► Electronic information boards

- Which languages do materials need to be produced in to serve the needs of stakeholders? What translation services are required for live events or meetings?

- What communication is needed at which frequency with the ecosystem partners to guide the ongoing development of the space and the wider Innovation District?

Staffing

What roles are required to deliver the objectives of this studio?

Role	Core Responsibilities	Skills/Experience/ Knowledge Required

Budget

- How much money is required to support the design, development, and ongoing operations of the Innovation Studio?

- Who is funding this budget?

- How long are the funds committed for?

- Which gaps exist in the budget, and what are the plans to close these gaps?

While the development of the Innovation Studio is still underway at the time of the writing of this book, following an ecosystem-centered approach to designing the studio will ensure that it turns into a truly valuable and supportive Beacon for the Downtown Mesa community.

If you are opening a physical space for your Beacon, you can download a Beacon planning template at https://pamelaslim .com/thewidestnet.

TILT PARENTING GOES FULL TILT

Due to the success of the Tilt Parenting podcast, Debbie got approached by an editorial director who had been turned onto her show, loved what she was doing, and wanted to know if she'd ever consider writing a book for parents. The editor had no idea that she had already authored books and was thrilled to know she was interested in writing a book about Tilt Parenting. Debbie got a book deal and published *Differently Wired: Raising an Exceptional Child in a Conventional World* with Workman Press Publishing in 2018.

With a growing social media platform of over 40,000 followers and her podcast in the top five podcasts in the world in her category, Debbie launched the Differently Wired Club in fall 2019 as a paid community membership. It continues to be her primary offering and a centralized place to support her community of parents of differently wired children. She also occasionally does one-off workshops with fellow parenting authors and experts, usually at low cost or a pay-what-you-will model to make them accessible. She continues to book paid speaking engagements at conferences, schools, and parent organizations. In March 2021, the Tilt Parenting podcast reached the milestone of three million downloads.

Having seen Tilt Parenting from the very beginning when our work started, I asked Debbie about her choice to choose her podcast as a primary Beacon:

> *The podcast was really everything. Because when I launched Tilt, I started at zero—no list, no social media following, no nothing. The podcast gave me a unique offering to share in other list-serves and communities I was in, created easy opportunities for amplifying and spreading the word, and gave people a chance to get to know me as a human. I think podcasting is a very personal medium, especially when the hosts are real and vulnerable and "in it" with their listeners. Establishing that accessible vibe right from the start was a critical piece of my community's growth, because listeners felt instantly connected to me and as if they were a part of something. And they inherently wanted to invite others to be a part of it, too.*

EXERCISE: Beacon Planning Template

My Primary Beacon is (check one):

☐ Email newsletter:

☐ Podcast:

☐ Blog:

☐ Regular meetup:

☐ Annual event:

☐ Social media satellite: (Write in which one: _____)

Do I also have a physical space? Yes/no

My Secondary Satellites are (Where will I cross-post content published on my primary Beacon? Circle all that apply.):

Twitter   Facebook   LinkedIn   YouTube

SnapChat   TikTok   Pinterest

Other: _____

What kind of content do I want to share on my Beacon? Check all that apply:

☐ Tips or how-tos

☐ In-depth stories

☐ Features of customers/clients

☐ Curated links from others

☐ Other: _____

What cadence will I share content on my Beacon?

Daily

Weekly

Bimonthly

Monthly

How will I align my business brand with the content shared on my Beacon? (Add notes in each category):

Brand voice:

Look/feel:

READY TO SELL?

For some reason, many small business owners love sharing useful content and building community around their Beacon, but get nervous thinking about moving relationships into the process of selling.

While the experience of sharing your point of view and solving problems is a really important part of your business operations, receiving money for your products or services is the thing that will sustain you and your business.

In the next chapter, you will see that selling can be an organic and relaxed experience with your ideal customers, and something that increases trust and connection, instead of severing it.

Fun while selling is not an oxymoron. You will see!

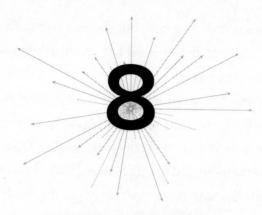

STEP EIGHT:
THE SALES YOU MAKE

*As sellers, if we are going to be successful
landing the big ones, we need to expand
our thinking about what's possible.*

—Jill Konrath

aryl Garcia grabbed a few minutes alone in the quiet of
the restroom to cry tears of frustration and exhaustion
when the stress became too much. As a 26-year-old archi-
tect in her home state of Cebu Island, Philippines, she had the
responsibility of managing one of the hardest projects of her life,
the five-year build of a Latter-day Saints temple. All her older
colleagues had quit the project in frustration with the exacting
details and she was the only one left with the skills to finish it.

"I was just so tired," she said, but she was committed to seeing the project through because she felt accountability to the client and knew no one else could do it.

On her way home one evening, she stopped by the mall and went into a bookstore. She was browsing for architecture books, but suddenly felt drawn to the business section. On a shelf at her eye level, turned out and facing forward was a book with a gray cover of cubicles with employees' faces poking out from behind the walls like prairie dogs.

"I didn't even read the back cover," she said, she just walked to the front counter and bought the book. That book was *Escape from Cubicle Nation*. As she read the book, something just clicked, and she began to dream about working for herself. Her parents thought she was crazy for leaving the stability of a good job in an architecture firm. But the seed for escape was planted.

She stayed with the temple build until it was done. But in the meantime, she registered three possible business names with the local government. They only approved one: Dream Architects.

One week before turning over the large, finished temple project, she was wrestling with continuing to work for her firm or going out on her own. "I was looking for a sign from God," Daryl said. An old client she had done work for in her employer's firm reached out to say they had referred her to a client who wanted her to pitch designing a seven-townhouse development. When she went in to do her presentation, she discovered she was one of 20 firms bidding for the project. They told her the name of the housing development: Dream Homes. She got the job. She had her sign. Dream Architects had its first client.

SELLING IS THE NEXT NATURAL STEP

Just about every client I have ever worked with has some form of angst about selling. Some feel like their natural relationship-building skills dissolve as soon as they start to talk about a concrete project with a prospective client. Others get flustered when preparing pricing for a proposal. Others are afraid of the murky process of asking for a decision and waiting for a sale. They distress over getting ghosted or being led on by a prospect until finally being told no.

I think the root of these fears, and many others, has to do with three main factors:

Mindset: You think that you have to become a different person or approach selling in a different way than you approach seeding and connecting.

Preparation: You don't go into a sales conversation with a grounding of information about your own mission or approach, and you don't research or prepare on your prospective customer.

Process: You don't have an understanding of the sales process and the steps involved, so you stumble and fumble your way through the sales cycle, and it feels vulnerable and awkward.

Getting comfortable with the process of selling and seeing it as a normal and natural part of doing business and building community is critical for achieving your business mission and creating a sustainable business. Developing into an effective salesperson is possible for those of you who have always told yourself, "I am allergic to sales," or "I never want to turn into one of those manipulative and pushy salespeople." I used to feel this way too, until mentors showed me a way to sell that was in alignment with my skills and strengths.

Set Your Mindset

What you think about selling will drive the experiences you have selling.

If you think: "I hate pressuring people into making a sale," then it is likely you view sales as pushing people to do something they don't want to do. Because you don't want to do that, you may swing to the other extreme and develop some really wiggly and uncomfortable interactions with your prospective customers.

If you think: "I have only two years being a (coach/consultant/entrepreneur/accountant/insert your title), so why would anyone want to pay me a lot of money to work with me?" Regardless of the fact that you are exceptionally great at what you do and get concrete results for your clients, if you focus on your inexperience, you likely will underprice your services and miss some sales opportunities because of your lack of confidence.

On the other hand, if you think: "I love this work so much I would do it for free, and I shouldn't really get paid for it," you might struggle to price your services in accordance with the value they create for your customers—and that could lead you into an unsustainable business model.

Selling is a natural and essential part of solving the core problem you are passionate about in your mission. Through all your work up to this point in the book, you have chosen a problem to solve that is deeply meaningful to you and the world. You have zeroed in on serving an audience with a problem you can uniquely solve, with your specific gifts, skills, and ingredients. You have created an offer that is the right solution. You are surrounded by peers and partners in your ecosystem who are equally committed to solving the problem of your ideal customer.

With this knowledge, it is critical to develop a sales mindset of service, pride, and confidence. Set your mindset by anchoring a core thought about selling that will direct the emotional experience you have throughout the process. Something like: "When I sell effectively, I allow my work to make impact on the lives of my ideal customers and deliver the exact value and results they are seeking."

Prepare for the Sales Process

A lot of what drives stress when you begin to engage with a prospective customer who expresses interest in doing paid work with you is worrying what you will say if they ask hard questions like:

- What kind of experience and outcomes do you have working with clients like me?

- What's the total price for this yearlong contract? (if you haven't scoped it out yet)

- How does your method specifically address issues in my industry?

- What kind of deal can we work out if I buy a large quantity?

- I am also considering working with (insert a competitor). How is your product different from theirs?

A lot of anxiety in the sales process will be reduced when you organize your sales information and develop useful documents, shortcuts, and answers to the most common questions you deal with in the sales process.

This includes:

- Client lists and case studies to demonstrate the work you have done with clients who fit your ideal customer profile and who purchased your core services. These case studies should show clear and tangible results, and satisfied customers.

- A clear pricing framework you can use to develop answers to specific questions, such as "My core service is $5,000 and that includes a complete set of illustrations you can use without restriction" or "Yearlong projects such as these range from $200,000–500,000 depending on these core five components . . ."

- Product comparison charts if you sell in a market with known and regular competitors. This should showcase how your product is preferable based on unique features, extra services, or superior support.

- Templates or proposal software that will make it easy to submit a proposal when you are at that stage of the sales process.

You also want to make sure you are clear about what your core offers are (based on work you did in Chapter 4), and what you do want and don't want to sell.

Manage the Sales Process

Twenty years ago, at the beginning of my consulting practice, I had a client named Skip Miller, author of *ProActive Selling*, who completely shifted the way I thought about selling. He explained that selling was simply helping your prospective customer walk through the steps they would normally take when making a buying decision, and then once that cycle was complete and they had all the information they needed, to request a decision, yes or no.

For example, if you watched the series *Outlander* and suddenly decided you needed to go to Scotland and stay in a castle, your buying process would go something like this:

- Start to Google "Castles for rent in Scotland" and look through a whole range of options.

- Determine your budget and prioritize what is most important to you, like location, room comfort, or the likelihood of running into a dashing Scottish suitor.

- Narrow down a list of potential locations.

- If you are going with other people, discuss specific dates that would work for all of you.

- Reach out and talk to each property to find out more information like amenities, activities nearby, and the reservation and cancellation process.

- Confirm you have the budget to make the trip.

- Make a final decision.

- Take out your credit card and book the reservation.

- Tell 100 of your closest friends you will be staying in a Scottish castle.

If you were the proprietor of a Scottish castle, you would want to match your sales process with the prospective client's buying process, so you would need to be prepared to ask questions like:

- Why are you excited to come to Scotland?

- What kinds of activities are you planning on doing when you are here?

- What is most important to you regarding accommodations?

- How many are in your party?

- When are the dates of your trip?

- How and when are you making your final decision?

You would also be prepared to show beautiful pictures of your castle rooms for rent, testimonials from satisfied customers, and perhaps a quote from *Outlander* star Sam Heughan saying, "There is no better and more authentic place for fans to get the true *Outlander* experience than this Scottish castle."

When your potential customer was ready to book their trip, you would have an easy and intuitive process to accept payment and follow-up materials to help them plan their trip.

Skip explained five steps in the sales process in his book *Pro-Active Selling*, 2nd edition[1]: initial interest, educate, transfer of ownership, rationalize, and decide.

Here is how I describe each step:

1. **Initial Interest.** When your potential customer expresses an interest in your product or service, and you both determine if there is a general fit between their need and your solution and it is worth it to continue talking.

2. **Educate.** A period of two-way education where you learn about the needs of your potential customer and they learn about your product or service.

3. **Transfer of Ownership.** When something "clicks" for your potential customer and they take ownership of the solution. It is that moment on a test-drive of a new car that a customer feels like "this is *my car.*"

4. **Rationalize.** Once excited by your product or solution, the buyer may second-guess their decision, reevaluating budget, wondering if they should talk to other vendors,

and questioning if now is truly the right time to invest with you.

5. **Decide.** When the buyer needs to make a decision, yes or no, without delay.

Knowing these steps in the sales process lets you plan for questions, develop helpful sales materials, and prepare your sales operations to make buying from you as simple as possible.

Having been in the online commerce world for 16 years, I know there are some models of online selling that don't require talking to potential customers. In this model, you still need to develop sales or landing pages to anticipate and address the questions that you know will arise as your buyer is evaluating your product or service.

Whichever method you use, it is critical that it is aligned with your values, congruent with your relationship-building approach all the way through the marketing process, and effective in communicating the true value of your product or service.

If you find yourself trying to coerce someone into working with you, it just means you have not done a good enough job in the sales process of determining their true needs, crafting a solid solution, and communicating the benefits of working with your company. Heavy-handed sales tricks that prey on the fears of your potential customer and manipulate them into making a decision before they are ready put both you and them in a compromising position. You will accomplish what most call "overcoming objections" by providing organized, useful, and helpful information and resources to answer your prospects' questions through the sales process.

Not all potential customers will choose to work with you. But those who do with purpose and agency will be shining examples for your brand and will drive lots of joy and business results.

SELLING THE DREAM

Daryl spent the first couple of years in Dream Architects working with the original client who hired her for the Dream Homes project. She maintained a clear focus on managing the design process tightly and producing high-quality work. This ethic led to them hiring her for multiple projects.

As she built her expertise designing different types of buildings, including shopping centers and theme parks, her reputation grew in the local area, and more developers became interested in working with her. She stayed closely connected to the professional groups that provided professional training and networking. As the projects grew, so did her team. Within 10 years, she had scaled to 53 employees, and designed and built her own four-story Dream Architects home base.

A commitment to excellence and to satisfying her customer's expectations was a big part of Dream Architects' growth, but so was Daryl's adherence to the mission. She cares about making dreams come true, whether for her employees or her customers. She had clients come to her saying, "We have been watching you for the past 10 years, and now that we have the funds to build our dream home, we know you are the only person to do this for us." She also knew when to say no to projects that were not in alignment with her values and mission.

When Covid-19 hit the Philippines, building projects slowed, and Daryl cut back her team to a core group of 12 to continue with the existing projects and ride out the pandemic. With a lighter workload, she quarantined with her family on a piece of land they owned and built Azienda Gracia, a sustainable eco-farm where she hosts outside guests, teaches them about organic farming, and harvests a bounty of fruits and vegetables.

Now that the world is slowly getting back to business, Daryl is overseeing her largest project to date: a 40-story condominium project in Mandaue City, Cebu. Because of her strong client relationships, excellent reputation, and loyal employee base, she can grow in the direction she chooses. "My main mission is to help people make their dreams come true," Daryl said. "I am happy to have many options, whether it is to expand my passion for organic farming or to grow my firm internationally."

REMOVING OBSTACLES TO SELLING EFFECTIVELY

So far, you have learned about developing a positive mindset toward selling, preparing information to help you answer prospective customer questions, and choosing a sales process that resonates with your values and style. Two remaining elements of selling will help ensure you have a viable business model and a realistic sense of how much incoming cash to expect: managing your sales pipeline and selecting your pricing model.

Manage Your Sales Pipeline

If I asked you, at this moment, how many opportunities in your sales pipeline were likely to close, what would your answer be?

1. A quarter?

2. Half?

3. All of them?

4. What's a sales pipeline?

Too Much Optimism

A lot of things go into generating and closing a lot of sales. I will talk about some in a moment. But before we get to that, I want you to know the biggest cause of sales pipeline clogging: *too much optimism.*

Here are common things I hear from my clients:

> "I really think this one will close because they said they were really interested."

> "We had a great vibe. I feel good about it."

> "I have no idea what happened. I was sure this project was going to happen. We had so many meetings. I was just informed they went with someone else. What am I going to do now?"

You need to have a huge amount of optimism and enthusiasm in business because it is the fuel that activates you doing the work you were put here on this earth to do. Use all of it when you make a great connection with a potential client who you know you can help. Give them a clear proposal and genuinely express your enthusiasm to work with them. Then, when you have done all you can do, let the rest gloriously go. Until their check clears your bank, consider that you have mediocre chances of closing this business, and continue seeding new opportunities. This attitude will give you so much more peace of mind and a much more accurate sense of pipeline.

The reality is, we often need 10 times the number of sales opportunities than we think we do to generate income stability and growth.

Five Fixes That Will Change Everything

A lot goes into the sales process. Here are five fixes that may help you sell more effectively.

1. Qualify, Qualify, Qualify

What questions do you ask in your sales process? Do you spend a lot of time getting to know what your clients are trying to accomplish, and why it is important? Do you know when they need to have that thing you are helping them do done? Exactly? What will happen if it doesn't get done?

Build a consistent list of questions for the beginning of your sales process to be sure you deeply understand the problem or challenge faced by your prospective client. Use this to build a clear and feasible solution, at a price resonant with the value and the financial resources of the client.

2. Simplify Your Proposal Process

About four years ago, one of the projects I worked on with Karley Cunningham from Big Bold Brand in her business turn-around was evaluating and improving her proposal process. She is a very thorough and detailed person and was spending about 20 hours on average with a larger consulting proposal. As business started to pick up again, she became extremely stressed when she had many proposals to generate at the same time.

She reengineered the entire proposal process and ended up reducing the time involved to a manageable two hours of work per proposal. Pairing extremely consistent marketing actions over time with her renewed rigor in her sales process, she ended up totally turning things around, to the point of having an overflow of work.

3. Don't Trust the Maybes

Skip Miller always says, "Yes's are great. Nos are great. Maybes will kill you." Believing that deals in your pipeline will close is the biggest killer of sales momentum, and frankly, your emotional well-being.

After talking with an ideal client, it is normal to get really excited about working with them. If you aren't careful, you can get ahead of yourself and actually believe you are already working with them and don't need to talk to anyone else.

A maybe is not a yes. Consider it a no. And go plant some more seeds.

4. Tell People What You Do, and Why You Love It

I work with many people who are generous and humble. They don't feel comfortable blasting everyone about how great they are all the time. Effective selling is not blasting people. Selling is, as my friend Phil Jones says in his audiobook *How to Persuade and Get Paid*, "Building enough trust to make a recommendation."

I hope you are in the kind of business that you believe in. I hope you truly get joy from doing the work. And I hope that you feel so excited when your clients have success that you can't wait to share it with everyone. If this is the case:

>   Do your neighbors know what you do?

>   Do your parents and friends know what you do?

>   Do your past clients, peers, and fellow employees have a clear sense of what you are doing now?

>   What benefit are you getting from withholding this information?

Tell them! And watch more opportunities appear.

5. Ask for a Decision

Your main goal in sales is not to get a close, but rather to get a decision, yes or no. If you don't have a decision, as Skip says, you have a maybe. Before you leave a sales conversation, define the next steps, check to make sure your prospective client is in a place to make a decision, then outline a specific date to make a decision. To respect both of your efforts and energy, you need to make a decision in a timely manner. If they don't respond to you in that timeframe, they have other priorities, and that is OK.

As for you, you have problems to solve, things to build, and people to help. Get out there and plant some more seeds.

PRICING OPTIONS FOR SERVICE-BASED BUSINESSES

Many of you may run a service-based business, such as coaching, consulting, accounting, law, or design. In this kind of business, it can be helpful to choose different frameworks for setting up your pricing structure. Because each business owner has a different style and set of values, there is not one right pricing structure, just the one that works for you and your customers.

Here are some pricing structure options:

- **Retainers:** You are paid a fixed amount for a weekly, monthly, or yearly time span. You spell out exactly what is covered in your retainer agreement.

- **Daily rate:** You estimate the number of days your offer will take, and you charge by the day. (This, like all pricing structures, could be one component of various pricing options, put together in a project proposal.)

- **Time and materials:** This is the easiest to track and bill, but leaves you tied to trading time for money and opens you to negotiation with the client about how much time it takes for you to complete the project. The better and faster you get at your delivery, the less you make, which is not building value in your business. That said, it is a common starting structure for new service professionals who do not know exactly how long a task may take to complete.

- **Fixed fee:** This is very common in large companies, where they want to contract for a fixed fee. To use this pricing structure, you have to have a good handle on what it takes to deliver a project.

- **Performance-based fee:** In certain situations, it can be advantageous to tie your fee to the client results. The upside to this strategy is profiting from positive client outcomes. The downside is that you may not have control over how the project is implemented and sustained, putting your income at risk.

- **Value-based pricing:** This type of structure was popularized by Alan Weiss, who has contributed a great number of ideas and intellectual property in this area through books like *Million Dollar Consulting*. He ties fees to the value of client outcomes, not time and materials to deliver the outcome. See more on his methodology at https://pamelaslim.com/thewidestnet.

TRUE VALUE IS BUILT OVER TIME

A flourishing business and respected brand are built by:

- How clearly you define and understand our audience

- How well you articulate and represent the problems you solve

- How well you do your work

- How well your articulated values match the experience your clients have with you (personally and professionally!)

- How well your business operations create a smooth and seamless experience for your clients

- How well you keep your promises

- How clearly your visual and written brand assets convey your value

When you do these things right, selling becomes easy.

EXERCISE: Sales Checklist

I am here to solve this problem for my ideal customer (from Chapter 3):

Mindset:
The thought that anchors my mindset for selling is:

Preparation:
I have prepared the following items and identified the following core offers to engage in a sales process:

- Determined pricing structure

- Created proposal template
- Got case studies or testimonials from past clients
- Created informational materials for use in the sales process
- Implemented clear process for receiving payment
- Finalized agreements and contracts

Process:

I will ask the following questions of each prospective customer at different stages of the sales process:

Beginning

Middle

End

Onboarding

These are the critical steps I need to take to onboard a new customer:

EXPAND THROUGH PARTNERSHIPS

If you have completed the exercises in each chapter and taken your tiny marketing actions (TMAs) seriously, people will start to appear who are interested in working with you. Now that you have clarity about how to have a successful sales experience with these people so they turn into customers, you are in a good place to build strong referral and joint venture partnerships to expand your audience even further.

In preparation for this stage, this next chapter provides a framework to carefully select the best partners and slowly and methodically cultivate effective working agreements.

STEP NINE:
THE PARTNERSHIPS YOU FORM

*Partnership is giving, taking, learning,
teaching, offering the greatest possible benefit
while doing the least possible harm.*
—**Octavia E. Butler,** *Parable of the Talents*

I n 2016, Hajj Flemings invited Automattic's John Maeda
to speak at Brand Camp University in Detroit, Michigan.
(Automattic develops WordPress, the world's most popular
content management software.) Flemings, a branding expert,
was passionate about eradicating the digital divide between
those with the skills and access to take full advantage of the

internet and those who still struggled with systemic barriers to this critical tool. He'd created the event to gather thought leaders, technologists, professional marketers, and creatives to discuss branding and entrepreneurial thinking around preparing people and cities for the new world of work. Maeda, whose mandate as global head of computational design and inclusion lined right up with this mission, happily agreed to attend.

WordPress plays a major role in the creative economy, powering 35 percent of the world's websites. Automattic's software provides entrepreneurs with foundational tools for e-commerce, brand awareness, thought leadership, and creative expression. While the demand for website software is endless, the competition is relentless.

With Black-, Latinx-, and women-led businesses among the fastest-growing segments of the small business economy, Maeda knew that Automattic needed to do more than simply run ads. To grow into these new markets, they needed to build partnerships with organizations and individuals that understood the unique needs and challenges of these communities. While in Detroit for the event, Maeda wanted to learn more about the local entrepreneurial scene, especially in these growing demographic segments.

"I was excited to bring John around to our big shiny projects in the suburbs, where universities were working on big academic initiatives in tech," Hajj told me. But Maeda wasn't interested in the big economic development initiatives sponsored by city officials or well-funded institutions. He already understood the needs of suburban WordPress users. He wanted to explore inner-city Detroit to get a sense of the issues its business owners faced. So Flemings brought Maeda around the city to meet with everyone from barbers to café owners to artists. This experience marked the beginning of a grand partnership to get urban businesses online: Rebrand Cities. In their initial research, Flemings and Maeda discovered that a whopping 46 percent of small businesses in the United States don't even have a website, let alone a well-designed one. (For a company offering a platform to easily build websites, this represents a staggering amount of market potential.)

Rebrand Cities got underway with a small pilot in Detroit. Over a weekend in 2017, a team of 10 WordPress developers spent 12 hours building websites pro bono for 10 local entrepreneurs. The developers were excited to learn firsthand about the specific needs of these business owners. The business owners, meanwhile, were eager to finally have an online presence. At the end of the day, 10 new websites meant 10 businesses could engage with customers in a new way and take advantage of digital marketing to grow.

For Hajj Fleming, Rebrand Cities brought his vision of closing the digital divide one step closer. For Automattic, it offered exposure to a market it had previously only understood in broad demographic terms. They learned firsthand how lean mom-and-pop budgets are and how overwhelming it can be for someone who is new to the internet to tackle even the basics of using WordPress. The insights it gained in the heart of these Detroit neighborhoods, guided respectfully by its experienced and trusted partner Hajj Flemings, gave the company a new window into a giant market of potential customers.

Partnerships like Rebrand Cities are at the heart of the ecosystem model. To find watering holes teeming with ideal customers, you need to create strong, vetted partnerships with other players in the ecosystem who have built authentic relationships with your ideal customers. Unfortunately, most business partnerships are formed in a casual, transactional way. In the moment, working together always sounds like it has nothing but upside. But over time, you often begin to regret your split-second decision-making. Ecosystem partnerships cannot be transactional. They must exist on a sturdy foundation of research, communication, and experience. A partner with a strong brand and an excellent reputation in their community should never risk that reputation to partner with an unvetted person or organization.

The strength of an ecosystem lies in its connective tissue and respectful and authentic partnerships. You trust each other deeply and refer clients to each other willingly. You are excited to invite your partners to the stage in front of your customers because you know that what they have to share will be deeply valuable to them. You promote products you know will solve the problems your business can't address itself.

This is not a loose net of tenuous connections; it is a fabric that strengthens with each strand of interdependence. The key is *we all need each other*—I need you as much as you need me. Together, we form an unbroken net of insight, support, solutions, and value to our customers.

BUILDING GREAT PARTNERSHIPS

In 2009, I attended the South by Southwest (SXSW) conference in Austin, Texas. At the time, SXSW was the ultimate watering hole for tech companies and entrepreneurs as well as those who serve them. At an evening event, I met Charlie Gilkey, a young business coach whose gentle nature, warm smile, and grounded presence immediately won me over. As we began discussing our coaching work, I learned more about his unusual background. Growing up, he'd been both an Eagle Scout and a high school cheerleader. Later, while a doctoral candidate in philosophy, he became a logistics officer in Iraq with the US Army. Now, he was helping entrepreneurs navigate business complexity, developing systems that provided order, structure, and rhythm to their processes. While we worked with overlapping demographics, we provided very different kinds of support to our clients. Our own demographics were different, too: I'm middle-aged and white, he's a decade younger and Black. In every sense, we complemented each other.

Charlie and I began a series of regular discussions to learn more about each other's practices. Eventually, we explored the idea of building a program together, and a few months later, Lift Off was born: a four-day immersive retreat for new entrepreneurs.

We held the inaugural Lift Off in Phoenix for 15 brave participants and, over the next three years, ended up working with six cohorts. The alumni went on to found companies, grow seven-figure practices, and build partnerships with some of the biggest thought leaders in the world. They formed alliances and partnerships with each other and made big impacts in their communities. A decade later, Lift Off alumni still tell us it was one of the most impactful events they have ever attended.

Working with Charlie was deeply gratifying. Our core values were in alignment and we filled crucial gaps in each other's areas of competence. When we finally decided that Lift Off had run its course, we shuttered it amicably and continued on our solo paths. Today, Charlie and I remain good friends and peers despite the fact that we often target the same potential clients. It isn't even uncommon for someone to explore working with both of us. When that happens, we collaborate on creating the right fit, regardless of who benefits financially. In the end, it's more important for each of us to know that clients are getting exactly what they need.

Building great partnerships like ours is a crucial part of widening the net, but it's fraught with risk if you don't adopt a good process. The process that follows has served me and my clients well. The amount of time it takes to complete each of these steps depends on the size of the endeavor—from collaborating on a small joint venture to setting up a multiyear referral partnership—but the steps themselves remain the same. Each one is essential to ensuring a healthy and productive partnership for both sides.

1. Define Your Service as a Problem Solved

In Chapter 3, you identified your ideal customer in terms of one or more specific problems you want to solve for them. For example, if you own a pool-cleaning service, this might be "a busy homeowner who prides herself on a clean, tidy living environment but hates to do the work herself." If you're an attorney specializing in intellectual property, your ideal customer might be "a marketing agency that wants to create compelling content for clients without getting sued." Avoid demographic definitions of customer segments when first defining your ideal customer. The fact that your pool cleaning customer makes $150,000 a year or works in the oil and gas industry may be useful down the road, but it won't lead you to an ideal ecosystem partner. An ideal ecosystem partner is identified through the main problem you are solving: delivering her a clean, tidy living environment.

Once you define your ideal customer by their specific problem or challenge, you are ready for the next step: finding other people who solve this problem in a complementary way.

2. Look for the Jelly to Your Peanut Butter

Who offers a product or service that is highly complementary to yours? Partnerships should be so highly correlated that the connection is obvious to everyone. For example, graphic designers who help their clients communicate concepts with images need copywriters who help their clients communicate concepts with words. An accountant's clients also need lawyers. Busy homeowners who hire a service to clean their pool also hire people to clean their house and trim the hedges in their yard. The jelly to your peanut butter should offer an extremely obvious and essential complement to your offering.

A good way to identify these natural partners now that you've identified the core problem you solve is to write down the answers to the following question: "What else would be necessary to solve this problem?" For example, if you help your customer have a clean, tidy swimming environment by cleaning her pool, what else might need to be cleaned and tidied?

From there, brainstorm: her yard, her windows, her closet, her refrigerator, her car, her driveway, even her computer. Then ask yourself: "Which kinds of people could help her clean these areas of her environment?" Your answers might include a landscaper, a housecleaner, a professional organizer, a tech consultant, even a nutritionist, if you think of clean eating as part of your definition of a clean and tidy environment. Now your job is to identify and connect your ideal customer to these professionals and introduce yourself to the ones who are already working with her. They might be working in homes and neighborhoods you don't have access to, an opportunity to widen your net.

3. Date First

Your biggest risk when partnering is moving too fast. You would never propose marriage on a first date. Likewise, your first interactions with a potential partner should be calm and cautious. Take your time to get to know your partner across different environments. Observe their habits:

- Are they late to meetings?

- Do they step aside on sidewalks to let people pass?

- Are they constantly looking at their phone?

- How do they talk about their loved ones, if they talk about them at all?

- Do they return your calls or texts promptly?

- How do they respond to feedback?

- Do they hit their deadlines? If not, do they blame someone or something else for the delay instead of taking ownership for their actions?

All of these considerations and more are indicators of your potential partner's character, which itself is a major predictor of the success of any partnership. Remember, you aren't just looking for a partner whose work is a natural complement to yours (like a graphic designer and a copywriter), you're looking for someone whose work process is highly aligned with your values, work style, and the needs of your customers. Be thorough. Actions speak louder than words. As you get to know your potential partner better, follow up on your initial hunches with more observation. It's easy to be so excited about the potential upside of a partnership that you turn a blind eye to potential red flags.

4. Do Your Due Diligence

Personal chemistry can be wildly misleading. A "good feeling" about a partnership should be verified by the transparent sharing of information with each other. Each partner should feel comfortable asking for specific data to validate the hunch that there will be a benefit in working together. Some of the information that can be helpful in evaluating a potential partnership includes:

- Social media profiles

- Interviews with past partners or clients

- Business financials

- Legal documentation (sample contracts)

- Business policies

- Website copy

- Business plans

- Any past financial or legal issues (Have you ever gotten in
  serious financial trouble or been sued?)

You can both decide the level of detail that feels comfortable and reasonable to share at the due diligence stage. If you
are exploring a partnership with a much larger organization (as
when Hajj Flemings, an individual branding consultant, partnered with Automattic, a large tech company), it's unlikely you'll
need information like the entire company's detailed financials.
But many other areas of due diligence will be critical. What is
their brand reputation? Can you interview past partners to see
what their experience was? Examine their legal contracts. Do
they demonstrate respect and equity for smaller partners?

Beware of a potential partner who refuses to share or discuss *any* business information or has the need to tightly control
conversations with past clients or partner organizations. Also,
beware of someone who says you can "figure out the intellectual
property and financial details later."

A trusted ecosystem partner with nothing to hide will create
a reasonable plan for information sharing and will not be flustered by any discussion of information relevant to a potential
partnership. Just because one or both partners have had issues

in the past does not preclude future partnerships of value. Both must be willing to discuss what happened, what they learned, and what measures are now in place to make sure they don't happen again.[1]

5. Explore Your Drivers

Great partnerships are sustained not only by the economic benefit to each—foundational in any business relationship—but by each partner continually behaving in accordance with their shared values.

"Shared values" does *not* mean you share every interest. Desiree Adaway and I have been best friends for 35 years. Over the decades, we've done multiple joint-venture projects together. Yet there are very few things we both enjoy.

- She hates pop culture. I dance unabashedly to Bruno Mars.

- She has never seen a *Star Wars* film. Yoda is my adopted grandfather.

- She adores the perfect gin and tonic on a summer's day. I don't drink alcohol.

- She winds down in the evening by reading books with titles like *Black Against Empire: The History and Politics of the Black Panther Party*. I watch *Moonstruck* on Amazon Prime for the 50th time.

And yet we are both driven by the same fundamental desire: to build equitable and inclusive organizations, communities, and economies. That's what makes our partnerships work so well. When important questions arise—how to deal with an unhappy customer, how to improve product quality, when a product is ready to ship, when and how to pursue investment—our shared values come into play.

6. Define Partnership Goals

Before deciding on which project to partner on, ask yourself why you want to partner in the first place. Defining partnership goals will ensure that you choose projects, roles, and responsibilities that align with those goals. Here are some examples:

- Expand audience by comarketing.

- Create a piece of shared content.

- Enter into a new market.

- Leverage resources and trust built in each partners' community.

- Cocreate an event.

- Create a referral pipeline.

- Attract capital through grant partnerships.

Precise definitions of goals and partnership roles are critical and can have serious consequences if mishandled. A close friend of mine, who chooses to remain anonymous, shared this story of a partnership gone bad:

I tried to run a sales consultancy with someone who falsely claimed to have sales experience (I thought I was bringing the marketing). We had one client agree to a $25,000 deal—once she'd negotiated it (without me) down to a 90 percent discount. Then she gave them an extra 10 percent off that because her sales mentor had told her "you always discount for payment in full."

At the end of the six-month trial period, she moved 85 miles away and applied for a job copying my LinkedIn profile onto her résumé and listing me as her reference. A potential employer called me and listed all the good things she had done—which were all the good things I had done. When they finished rattling off my résumé, I told them that was my résumé, not hers, and they could validate it on my LinkedIn profile. Then I told them I'd be happy to take the job and started one day after our six months were up.

Sadly, stories like this are all too common. Here's one that's even worse:

My old business partner booked "business development" trips and meetings for nearly two years . . . and they were all phantoms. Not a single real opportunity, not a single contract signed. He simply paid himself to travel around and visit people he knew. Three years of that and we burned through all of the money I'd put in. Every dollar that came into that biz was my doing. He *was supposed to pay back 50 percent of the investment (we were 50/50 partners) from the proceeds selling his "other" business . . . and it turned out that that business wasn't a business either, just a handful of freelance clients he transitioned off. There was nothing sold, no assets, no money, no nothing. Air. I couldn't even sue him because there was nothing to sue for. In short, he was a total con artist, and it took me three years and nearly $300K to learn it!*

7. Test the Waters

Even if you see tremendous potential in a business partnership, always start off with a small test project. Choose a project that:

- Poses a limited risk to both businesses

- Lasts a relatively short time

- Allows each partner to demonstrate their particular skills and strengths

- Promises at least a few bumps in the road so you each can see how the other side handles pressure

For example, if you see an opportunity to build a new learning platform with a partner, start by creating one, short course. Through the process of designing and delivering it, you will learn what it's like to work together and whether you both want to continue to a more ambitious project.

8. Everyone Signs Something

My lawyer, Kyle Durand, has seen just about every type of partnership gone bad in his two decades of legal practice. That is why his first piece of advice to anyone entering a partnership is: "Everyone signs something." Each and every business arrangement should begin with a signed agreement, even for a "simple" project. That means you sign something if you:

- Produce an ebook together.

- Cocreate an event.

- Produce a webinar.

- Do any business activity that entails collecting business information, marketing, or creating new intellectual property.

Essentially, if you are doing anything at all related to generating revenue, collecting or sharing customer information, or creating intellectual property, draw up an agreement to protect both sides, and beware of any partner that resists this step. Critical elements of such an agreement include:

- What funds or in-kind services will be contributed by each partner?

- How will intellectual property be shared? Will both parties own their own IP? Will one have to ask permission of the other to use the IP in another form?

- How will payment be shared? How will percentages be calculated?

- How and when will payments be made to partners?

- Will there be a unique business entity for the partnership? If not, whose business entity will track and report on the financials?

- What will the project budget be?

- What will the decision-making process be?

- What will the exit clause be if either partner decides to exit for any reason?

9. Build Continuous Communication

Agree on a system of communication giving each partner full transparency into the status of every part of the work, including:

1. Project management

2. Financials

3. Customer relationship management

4. Intellectual property

The right system might include a combination of tools, from Dropbox for shared file storage to Asana for project management to Xero for accounting. It all depends on the specific needs of each partner, the project as a whole, the tools they already use in their own businesses, their IT policies, and so on. That said, communication tools are no substitute for actual *communication*. Well-designed and efficient meetings are a critical part of making any partnership work. Schedule opportunities at regular intervals for all key stakeholders to connect, and be sure to designate who will take notes or record conversations for the record.

10. Evaluate and Invest in the Relationship Regularly

Just because you've had a successful partnership for a period of time does not mean things will continue that way indefinitely. Set up specific check-in points to ensure that each partner is still satisfied with every element of the partnership, including:

- **Financial results.** Is the amount of profit aligned with each side's plans and goals?

- **Work output.** Are you each creating content or services that contribute to your individual and collective bodies of work, as well as to the ecosystem as a whole?

- **Impact.** Are you making a difference with the community you're trying to reach?

- **Process.** Does working together leverage each side's unique strengths? Is it free of unnecessary stress and drama?

- **Opportunity.** Does the project meet a critical need in the market? Is it likely to continue producing value?

- **Fun and creativity.** Is the work enjoyable and energizing? Is it better doing it with a partner than without?

$\longleftrightarrow$

A CAUTIONARY EXAMPLE

The hearts of most seasoned entrepreneurs are scarred by failed partnerships of years past. Even with the best of intentions and lots of planning and due diligence, it is impossible to weed out all the unethical people or anticipate every style or values mismatch. That said, with the foundation of a good process, even a failed partnership can be a useful learning experience that doesn't destroy the preexisting relationship.

Brian Shea and Joel Louis were great friends and officemates in Boston. They each ran technical consulting businesses with a specialty, Brian in Salesforce implementation and Joel in internet sales funnels. After three years of overhearing each other's conversations, they began to discuss the possibility of working together.

Brian loved the business development and client relationship side of his business. Joel loved systems integration, automation, and hiring. Each was tired of running their business alone and carrying the weight of all decisions and projects. A partnership that leveraged each of their strengths seemed promising.

To begin, they wisely decided to start small with a single consulting project. Brian hired Joel to streamline his business operations and implement better systems. Along the way, they documented progress and defined shared financial targets. As they did this work, they also had conversations about a longer-term partnership and documented their ideas, goals, strengths, and weaknesses.

Once the initial consulting project was complete, they started a three-month trial period during which they would work together on some projects while still running their individual businesses. The trial started out strong, with both partners excited about the possibility of leaning on each other's strengths.

As they got into months two and three, however, they each began to feel some unease. Unlike Joel, Brian didn't believe that every problem could be solved with the right hire. He wanted to slow growth down to ensure they could continue to deliver an excellent customer experience. Sometimes, this meant personally resolving problems with clients instead of passing the job on to a less-experienced staff member.

Joel, meanwhile, chafed at the rate of growth this hands-on approach required. His strength was in scaling businesses quickly, and he was getting impatient with Brian's deliberate pace. Joel also had family challenges that sometimes required him to pull out of work at a moment's notice, even for extended periods. In his own business, he had built a team to handle these situations, but if he were to be the COO of a partnership with Brian, those sudden and extended absences would be problematic.

At the end of three months, they decided it was not worth risking their very strong friendship on a business partnership with conflicting goals. They now know for certain that despite their natural chemistry, friendship, and complementary skills, they do not have the ingredients of an effective partnership. And through it all, Brian and Joel still share an office and are better friends than ever.

Now just imagine if they had just shuttered the old iterations of their businesses and jumped in headfirst! A way to avoid most partnership calamities is to just slow down and try things out systematically. Never skip any of the steps in the process, *especially* "Everyone signs something!"

←——————→

THE REBRAND CITIES SUCCESS STORY

Building an effective partnership is no small feat, but it can be more than worth the effort. For example, after doing the initial events in Detroit, Hajj Flemings and Automattic expanded their partnership to other cities, flying in a photographer and branding team to help with the one-day website builds. That model became expensive, however, so they decided to incorporate a new role: local ambassadors who could mobilize local creatives and website developers. This added scope meant updating plans and changing roles. "It's been rocky figuring out the business model," Hajj told me. "Anytime you are dealing with a multinational company, the project has to be bigger than one market. Building in additional revenue streams is critical for the project's success."

As the project progressed and each side learned more about the market and customer expectations, they reviewed and updated their legal agreements carefully. After the first year, John Maeda, the project's champion, left Automattic, requiring Flemings to build relationships with team members who didn't have firsthand knowledge of the project's genesis. The departure of his in-house advocate was tough, but it forced him to construct a stronger business case for Rebrand Cities and to figure out how to execute its work more rapidly.

In the end, the partnership journey has been more than worth it for both sides. When Automattic debuted their first-ever television ads for WordPress, they created five commercials using the Rebrand Cities Detroit project as source material. Their existing base of tech-savvy developers and designers didn't really respond to the ads, but they weren't the target market. For the mom-and-pop business owners in the hearts of cities across the country, it was an opportunity to see themselves and their stories represented in the context of e-commerce and online marketing.

Since its inception, Rebrand Cities has expanded to nine US cities and has served over 500 business owners to date, with plans to accelerate the number of events in each city per year. In 2019, Hajj Flemings and WordPress signed a deal to continue and expand the partnership for two more years, adding new partner cities like our own Mesa, Arizona, at my Main Street Learning Lab. Project ambassadors in each city help identify business owners who need websites, funding partners who can contribute to the effort, and volunteer developers to help build the websites. Meanwhile, Hajj is expanding the business model and building additional revenue streams with project ambassadors like the CIO of the city of Los Angeles.

Hajj's long-term vision for bridging the digital divide is being accelerated by smart partnerships like Rebrand Cities. And Automattic knows that to meet the needs of an ever-growing, diverse customer base, it needs to work with partners like Hajj to steward their community engagement with cultural and local awareness, building trust, brand equity, and business opportunity along the way.

Stewardship of trust is critical once the hard work of entering a new community has been done. This becomes a greater challenge within an organization with people coming and going over time, as when John Maeda departed Automattic. How do you build the Ecosystem model into the fabric of your organizational culture to safeguard these authentic, trusting relationships—with vendors, partners, and customers—over the long term? We'll look at that challenge in our final chapter.

10

STEP TEN:
THE ECOSYSTEM YOU PROTECT

Nothing retains its original form, but Nature, the goddess of all renewal, keeps altering one shape into another. Nothing at all in the world can perish, you have to believe me; things merely vary and change their appearance. What we call birth is merely becoming a different entity; what we call death is ceasing to be the same. Though the parts may possibly shift their position from here to there, the wholeness in nature is constant."
—Ovid, *Metamorphoses*

I n 2014, on a trip to the San Francisco Bay Area, I met up with my friend Guy Kawasaki at a Silicon Valley coffee shop. Guy is a bestselling author and speaker, the former chief evangelist at Apple and the founder of the Remarkable People Podcast. I had met him in one of those very 2006 social media moments—on a whim, without knowing him, I emailed a post from my blog Escape from Cubicle Nation called an "Open Letter to CXO's Across the Corporate World." He shared it the next day on his blog and I had my only "gone viral" moment of my blogging career, with tens of thousands of shares and hundreds of comments.

It was at that moment that I formulated the concept of "watering holes"—in 2006, Guy's blog was the perfect online gathering place for people interested in all things entrepreneurship, innovation, Apple, and social change. By connecting with his audience, I met so many people who became collaborators, mentors, and clients.

As we ate breakfast, he told me about a new chief evangelist position he had taken at an Australian-based startup called Canva. Asking how he came across the opportunity, he said, "I do whatever Peg Fitzpatrick tells me to do." Peg was his colleague and social media strategist, who also was doing work with the company. At that point in 2014, Guy's goal was to help Canva get to two million subscribers.

Right away, he showed me the product and the features of what it could do. He handed me a Canva T-shirt, which I promptly featured in a picture of the two of us on social media. I was excited to try it out and signed up as soon as I got back to my hotel room (and I have been a subscriber ever since!).

Now, seven years later and with Canva at around 80 million subscribers and growing by tens of thousands daily, I wanted to get his perspective on accelerating and scaling a brand. Guy said: "I just did my small part. I don't take credit for the work the sales and marketing team did to grow this. I did my role of an evangelist, which is to do as it says in the description: spread the good word. There are many factors that made Canva successful. But by far, it's the quality of the product. It's not a guy."

What evangelism meant in Guy's early days at Canva was to use his extensive relationships and influence in Silicon Valley to get people excited about the product. "I would show up and talk to anybody who'd listen, but I think my best practice is just get to the demo as soon as you can. I don't believe in a lot of talking and telling the corporate story and all that kind of stuff. If the product is great, the corporate story then might matter. But if the product is crap, it won't matter how great the corporate story is. They want to use the tool that's easy and fast and powerful and does what they need it to do."

Having watched Guy build community and share his thought leadership over 15 years, I think he operates with a lot of natural discernment, although he says he has less strategy than we might think. In 2009, we were on a panel at South by Southwest for bloggers who had secured book deals. An audience member asked Guy, "How do people like me get my work in front of busy or famous people?" He answered: "Some people say I have the Midas Touch meaning anything I touch turns to gold. They have it wrong. I only touch gold."

I took this to mean he is constantly scouring the environment looking for people who are doing excellent work solving problems he and his clients are also interested in solving. If he finds something useful to his audience, he will share it. And if he is exposed to a product that he thinks is great, he just might sign up to evangelize it.

EXPANDING AND RENEWING YOUR ECOSYSTEM

You have heard a lot of stories throughout this book of business owners who have implemented the Widest Net Method and began to see a steady influx of new customers. When you implement tiny marketing actions (TMAs) consistently over a number of months, it is not unusual to experience a regular flow of opportunities and requests for proposals. Where you were stressed about not having any clients before, the stress can turn to feeling overwhelmed as you field interest and inquiries from new places while servicing your existing clients.

This period, while exciting, can also be perilous because if you do not organize, operationalize, and get some help, you risk tanking the goodwill that has been developed by delivering excellent service to your clients. I call this the "eye of the needle" phase, where you build, strengthen, and streamline your operations.

Another phenomenon that takes place at this stage is the "cocky and complacent mindset" when you suddenly either believe you never have to plant seeds again, or your success is evidence that you have 100 percent figured out your business and you are no longer open to feedback, growth, or challenge from your employees, partners, and customers. Both scenarios will eventually tank your business.

As you look at building a renewable and growing source of customers, which for some means doubling your business, and for others growing it by a factor of a 100 or 1,000 times, your job is to grow your leadership skills and build the operations of your business.

Let's clear some space first by understanding how to pass through the eye of the needle.

EYE OF THE NEEDLE

When your business is growing, there are so many things to get done, and crushing deadlines, and kids' homework, and dogs that need to be walked, and that thing called grocery shopping. It can feel like trying to squeeze a whole ball of yarn through the tiny eye of a needle.

There are stages of business where you just need to plod along every day to get things done. You don't need to create undue pressure for yourself or work ungodly hours, because to do so over an extended period of time will burn you out.

In the eye of the needle stage of growth, you *do* need to get a lot of work done in a short period of time. Because the nature of the eye of the needle stage is that there is a big, immovable deadline that involves more than just you. Your publisher needs your manuscript. You are at capacity and cannot take any more customers, until you create some group offerings. Your membership site is shedding members at an alarming rate because you are not addressing customer service issues in a timely manner.

Clear the Decks

Anything, and I mean anything, that is extraneous to your critical eye of the needle task needs to be whacked. Sunday dinner with Grandma? She will have to forgive you. That Homeowner's Association meeting? Hard pass. Fun projects that you love to work on? On the shelf. This is no time for fun! Clear everything that is not totally essential so you can focus on your eye of the needle tasks (really call in a lot of favors—someone else could drive your kid to school for once, your family can live on those cans of beans in the back of the pantry for a few days, or you can forgo showering for, I don't know, three to five days.)

With this freed-up time, you are ready to dig into your busines operations.

Too Busy to Organize

Operations consultant La'Vista Jones of Thirty One Marketplace says the most common refrain she hears from prospective customers is, "I would love to put in systems, but I am just too busy to do it." Yet if they let her peek under the hood of their business, she finds they are often manually scheduling appointments, creating bespoke proposals for every new prospect, sending contracts via email and waiting for a scanned copy back, creating invoices, and reconciling the books themselves.

STEP TEN: THE ECOSYSTEM YOU PROTECT   217

This adds up to hours, sometimes days, each week where they are frantically trying to keep up with hundreds of tiny details to run their business.

"It gets to the point," La'Vista says, "where they start to experience some dread when prospective clients say yes, because it means hunting through disorganized folders and email threads to get the latest version of documents to complete the customer onboarding. They can also miss critical steps like forgetting to get a client to sign a contract."

From the new customer's perspective, it opens up an opportunity for buyer's remorse. The sudden rush of excitement to make a purchase can turn into regret if the customer doesn't get a clear confirmation of payment, instructions for moving forward, and continued prompt responses from the seller.

To prevent this from happening, you need to anticipate what their questions will be, document the answers, then automate as much as you can.

THIRTY ONE MARKETPLACE OPERATIONAL KICKSTART

When preparing to welcome a lot more customers into your business, there are five key operational areas La'Vista Jones recommends you organize. If you have limited time, evaluate which of these five areas is causing your business the most problems and start with that first:

1. **Customer Onboarding.** How is a new customer welcomed into your business? What is all the information you need to get from them to deliver your product or service? What information do they need from you to get off to a great start? Organize this and automate as much as you can using technology.

2. **Process Documentation.** If you want to bring in staff support, you need to document the steps and processes you have in place to run your business. You don't have to write everything out in exhaustive detail; you can document quickly using a screen-share tool like Loom.

3. **Leverage Automation.** Now may be the time to implement a full customer relationship management (CRM) or project management tool so you don't have to remember to do each step manually. Once your processes are implemented and digitized, it can be as simple as pressing one button to start a sequence of content and document flow that is seamless to your customer and removes your need to send out documents manually.

4. **Hiring Plan.** After leveraging automation, note the tasks that would be most helpful to hire someone to help with. These can be tasks like:
    a. Scheduling (online schedulers can help, but are often not enough for high-touch service businesses)

   b. Client management

   c. Onboarding and offboarding for staff members

   d. Service delivery

5. **Customer Offboarding.** As your customer completes their engagement with you, how do you say thank you and create an excellent offboarding experience? You could create a process that:

   a. Summarizes highlights from the engagement

   b. Asks ideal customers for referrals

   c. Requests a testimonial or case study

   d. Sends a note or thoughtful gift

If you get these five areas of operations handled, you will free up time to commit to product improvement, business development, and overall business operations.

Find more tips and tools for organizing your operations at https://thirtyonemarketplace.com.

Metrics and Measurement

With a great customer experience nailed down, you now want to prepare a baseline of metrics and measurement so you can have the data you need to analyze your marketing efforts.

Christopher S. Penn is chief data scientist at TrustInsights.ai. His company helps their clients understand and solve complex data issues and set up the tech stacks and foundations of search engine optimization (SEO), social, and content marketing.

When setting up the foundation for a scaling business, Christopher says to start with mapping your key performance indicators (KPIs).

> *For most business owners moving from startup to scaling, you would start with the thing that will put you out of business if you don't address it, which is revenue. Then you work backwards and define the metric that immediately precedes revenue. If you're B2B, it's probably closed deals, right? If you are B2C, it would be e-commerce and shopping carts completed. Then you continue to work backwards to define the metric that feeds this metric, that feeds this metric, and you end up with a chain that mirrors your marketing operations funnel. And that's kind of what you want to keep in mind at each stage of your operations to follow. What's the number that tells you whether that stage is functioning correctly? It depends on what kind of business and depends on the kind of software you have available to you as well.*

As for tools, Christopher says every scaling business needs these four marketing tools:

1. Customer relationship management (CRM system)

2. Marketing automation

3. Marketing analytics

4. Reputation monitoring

The exact tools you choose will depend on your resources available, including budget, time, and your technical aptitude. Christopher says most businesses today use the Google Marketing Platform that includes Google Analytics, Google Tag Manager, and Google Data Studio.

For many business owners, even the task of backward metrics mapping could feel overwhelming if you are not familiar with it. This is why at this stage it is often a good idea to bring in a marketing analytics professional who can help you define your initial KPIs, set up your core marketing tools, and plan for regular monitoring to evaluate trends.

LEADERSHIP GROWTH AND STAGES

With your operations better organized, measured, and automated, it is now time to focus on your growth as a leader so you exercise and build the skills to manage a growing organization. I always take pause when asked in interviews (now hundreds of times) "What skills are most important for being a successful entrepreneur?" Perseverance? Analysis? Negotiation? Sales? Finance?

My answer is usually some version of "All of them" and "It depends." The skills required for you to be successful in business have a very tangible side to them—all businesses require operational strength, marketing savvy, emotional intelligence, financial literacy, systems thinking, and sales skills.

There is also a very personal side to skills development as a business owner—the leadership skills you must exhibit and own to provide what your business needs from you.

This is the greatest source of angst, and also the greatest source of relief, for navigating challenges at different stages of growth. The leadership skills and perspective that get you launched in business are not the same as those that will get you through more mature stages of growth. Here are four key leadership skills that match phases of small business growth:

1. Grit and Determination

Half of my life, I have helped people take action on ideas that have been in their head for years, like starting a business, changing careers, or radically changing their lifestyle. To get momentum to take the first step toward such changes, most of what is needed is good old grit. The kind where you close your eyes and hit "publish" on your first blog post. Or the courage to walk into an unfamiliar networking event and steel your smile, stumble through your introduction speech, and hand over your slightly sweaty business card.

Precision and craft do not belong at this first phase—it is about action and forward movement.

LEADERSHIP GROWTH QUESTION: What can you do to develop more grit?

2. Discernment

When opportunities start to land, instead of saying yes to everyone with a pulse and a purchase order, you need to develop some decision criteria. If you say yes to every opportunity, then you risk becoming overwhelmed. You need to put operations and policies in place. You can't afford to throw money at problems anymore, so when you make big decisions like hiring, you need to take your time to hire the best candidate.

From an audience definition perspective, you need to get more and more clear about who are ideal and nonideal clients for you. Update your materials to be focused on the right clients.

LEADERSHIP GROWTH QUESTION: How can you be more discerning with business decisions?

3. Objectivity

When your business starts to grow and you gain more visibility and popularity, prepare for pushback, challenge, or outright rejection. At this stage of growth, you must develop thicker skin to not take challenges personally. If you want your business to grow and remain viable, you must develop comfort with handling difficult conversations. You must remain open to new perspectives if they mean changing ineffective processes and discovering new opportunities.

LEADERSHIP GROWTH QUESTION: How can you become more objective when receiving tough feedback?

4. Courage

The more years you are in business, the easier it is to get stuck in habits and patterns. You have more to lose, and you might fear destroying what you have spent so many years building. But it is at this stage of maturity that you are able to take a more active role as a mentor, both to employees and to others in the outside world.

To remain viable, you have to have the courage to explore new avenues and possibilities. To remain relevant, you have to decide when and how you will speak up in the public arena about issues that affect you, your customers, and your community.

Remember that at this stage of your leadership growth, you have already practiced grit and determination, discernment, and objectivity. These skills will help you be courageous in intelligent and effective ways.

LEADERSHIP GROWTH QUESTION: Where and how do I want to be more courageous as a leader?

Knowing where you are on your business and personal journey will help you know which leadership skills to develop. When you know where you are, you can balance not getting ahead of yourself with not staying stuck in the past.

SAFE, SEEN, HEARD, AND HONORED

We have explored a lot of marketing tools and tactics that will put you in front of people (speaking, Facebook ads, blogging, Instagramming), but how do you go from being casually linked to someone as a Facebook friend to actually being connected on an emotional level?

In implementing the Widest Net Method, people need to feel the following four things to truly feel part of your community: safe, seen, heard, and honored.

Safe

Does your business provide physical and emotional safety for your customers? Will people who engage with you know that you are concerned with their safety? This can show up as:

- Thinking about the experience someone will have getting to your live event.

- Thinking about how people in your community may treat someone who they perceive as different.

- Stepping in clearly and decisively if someone is being personally attacked in comments on a post, Facebook group, or in live conversation.

- Maintaining confidentiality in private conversations.

I want to stress that "safe" doesn't have to imply "always comfortable." Some of the very best community building involves real discomfort as people explore beliefs and perceptions, challenge assumptions, and explore differences.

Seen

Do your community members see themselves reflected in the images, stories, and examples you share about your business?

Do they see members of their community featured and honored as experts in yours?

This can show up as:

- Thoughtfully selecting speakers and experts for your live and virtual events.

- Sharing case studies and stories of the wide range of your customer and community base in your speeches and writing.

- Sharing and promoting the work of peers, partners, customers, and collaborators on social media, not just your own work.

- Actively promoting and/or sponsoring events and projects in communities that you want to connect with, without being asked or prompted. This is because you have taken the time to follow the work being done, because you believe in it and want to see it spread.

Heard

Do you stop and deeply listen to what your community is saying to you? Do you honor the lived experience of people in your community and not try to talk over them or tell them why their perceptions are not correct?

This can show up as:

- Being fully present and looking directly in someone's eyes when you meet them at a conference, and not looking over their shoulder to see if there is someone else more important or more interesting to talk to. (Has this ever happened to you? It is so frustrating and humiliating. I have made this mistake in the past and really practice being present when I meet people now.)

- Taking feedback to heart and changing policies, approaches, programs, or pricing so it meets the needs you hear from your community.

- Not being defensive when someone takes issue with your approach or your work. You can listen deeply, reflect back what you hear, decide what feedback you will take to heart, let the rest go, and sincerely thank the person for taking the time to communicate with you.

- Not mocking or ridiculing people who disagree with you. I see far too often on Facebook business owners who write "rants" about demanding clients or prospects. Whenever I see that, I always think, "I wonder if they realize that now every current customer and prospect they work with will think they are talking about them." And then they may fear that if they raise an issue or ask the wrong question, they may be mocked or ridiculed too (even if you don't call someone out by name, people will read between the lines). This is not a good strategy for building trust and safety in your community.

Honored

A true community is one where each person feels honored and valued as an equal member. Regardless of age, experience, income level, position of authority, or background, each person is valued for what they bring to the group. The goal of building community is not to create a homogenous group of people who all think and act the same, it is to create a diverse, stimulating, engaged group of people who are committed to solving problems together, in an environment of mutual respect.

This can show up as:

- Designing events to be interactive.

- Featuring a range of ideas and opinions from your community.

- Treating all members of your community with dignity and respect, including the natural environment surrounding your events (clean up after yourselves!).

Weirdo in the Room

Fundamentally, Widest Net leaders want to constantly explore new markets so they develop an uncanny ability to be the "weirdo in the room." Instead of clustering with the same group of friends who all promote each other's stuff for years on end in a tightly controlled environment with rigid rules for participation (mostly requiring that you promote each other's stuff even if you don't necessarily think it works), Widest Net leaders look for places where they can learn as much as they can from customers who have problems that interest them.

The Ecosystem Map gives you all kinds of clues for places to look for interesting watering holes.

- You might be the only graphic designer at a personal chef convention.

- You might be the only life coach at a funeral directors' association meeting.

- You might be the first insurance agent to appear on a podcast about robotics.

But if you can show up and *listen first*, then contribute your unique perspective on solving their problem, you could find a rush of new clients.

- The graphic designer could create a suite of menu templates for personal chefs.

- The life coach could promote their book *Recovering from Loss* as part of a package funeral directors could provide for their grieving customers.

- The insurance agent could promote a helpful risk management policy for promoters of robot competitions.

Being temporarily uncomfortable as the weirdo in the room may feel awkward and difficult at first, but you will survive. Over time, you will look forward to it.

CONNECTING AUTHENTICALLY AT SCALE

When you are communicating with hundreds of customers or connections, it is possible to build a personal relationship with many. When your community grows to tens of thousands and even millions, you need to organize your communication in a different way.

Caleb Gardner is the cofounder and managing partner of 18 Coffees and former digital director for Organizing for Action (BarackObama.com). Knowing he has managed large-scale communication for most of his career, I asked him how he advises companies to maintain a relational feel with their community and customers as they deliver content one to many. Caleb said:

> *I usually ask brand managers to imagine a series of concentric circles, with their most passionate brand advocates in the center, and the rest of us at varying levels of affinity outside of that, and the last and largest circle being the masses who've never heard of you. At each level, people want to be engaged with differently. When we're on the outside, you have to give us a reason to pay attention. When we've participated in a small way, we need to be encouraged to participate in a big way. And when we've proven to be mission-aligned, we need to have our loyalty rewarded. Most brand managers have more data now than ever to understand our history with their company, but most are still thinking about segmentation in terms of demographics and psychographics, not in terms of how we've raised our hand and signaled that we care.*

In his latest venture, 18 Coffees, a strategy firm devoted to building the backbone of the mission economy[1] through consulting, content, and community, partnerships are a central focus of the business. Caleb and his cofounder Robin Chung focus on creating peer-to-peer value between partners who are all working together toward the same cause. These are Caleb's three recommendations for connecting authentically at scale:

1. Be very intentional about storytelling as you grow. The visuals, rituals, and fables that take form when you're small help form your company lore when you're big.

2. Hone in on what makes your company great, why your customers are obsessed with you—and then document and systematize that as you grow. We talk about culture like it's a tool, but it's actually an outcome.

3. People talk about having a customer obsession, but I think it's becoming more important to have a community obsession—one that recognizes the importance of customers, employees, vendors, supply chain, and beyond in your sphere of influence. When buying your product contributes to something greater than your bottom line, there's more emotional resonance when making a very functional purchasing decision.

OPPORTUNITY STACKS

With operations whizzing and new markets being explored, you should aim to get the most out of every single business development opportunity, which I call "stacking." Stacking is the deliberate process of looking for ways that a singular marketing activity can be leveraged by "stacking" other opportunities for reach, exposure, or impact on top of it.

For example, if you are going to take the time to do a live talk about your core area of expertise at a local setting, why not stack getting photos and a video of the event on top of it? Why not livestream the talk for your nonlocal prospects? Why not arrange to meet a strategic attendee for coffee or dinner after the event? When you look for all the possible ways to maximize a marketing activity in your business, you will have a much better return on your investment of time, energy, and resources.

Here's a stacking example. In 2017, Susan Baier, Chris Lee, and I completed *Crack the Challenge Code*, a small business survey that looked at the attitudes small business owners have toward obstacles. This research is essential to do a better job in our respective businesses, since most of what our clients struggle with is not *what* to do (we all know we should market more consistently, write great content, build our product funnels, etc.), but few know *how* to do it (we get in our own way by becoming overwhelmed, feeling imposter syndrome, sticking our heads in the sand, etc.).

Putting together and executing a study of this size takes a significant amount of time, energy, and money. Knowing that, here are the stacks we used in this research project:

- Partnered with over 100 people and groups to spread the word about the survey.

- Designed the data collection to include both essential questions that will help business owners, but also questions that will help small business providers.

- Included research for a new book in the survey data.

- Secured a webinar with a small business web partner that highlighted the survey data to their thousands of customers.

- Designed our survey output to directly feed into the research needed to design our offerings.

- Designed our survey questions to be directly helpful to our local small business ecosystem planning, our local government, and our nonprofit and business partners that must make great decisions about resource allocation and program design.

- Chose a topic that has multiple dimensions and will be a great foundation for our content ideas for next year.

EXERCISE: Stack Your Opportunities

Look ahead to this quarter. What unique opportunities do you see?

- **What type of business development activity am I focused on this quarter?**
- **Select the stacking opportunities: How can I expand the impact of this activity by adding the following things:**

  Partnership. Who else might want to participate in this activity with me and work together to expand opportunities for both of us?

Press coverage. Is there a great story or press event that I could use to extend the impact of this activity?

Operationalize design. If this activity looks like a core part of my marketing strategy moving forward, how can I design it to be easily replicated the next time I do it (by creating checklists, using merge fields on communication, repeating launch processes, etc.)?

Use as an example in a newsletter article, blog post, or video. How can I highlight this work in multiple places?

Link to past articles/videos/podcasts to leverage that content. How can you include links to past work you have done to get more mileage from the content and increase audience engagement?

Have a photographer/videographer document you doing it. If you are doing a live talk, can you get a photographer and/or videographer to cover it so you can use the footage in future marketing materials?

Invite prospective clients/partners to attend so they see you in action. Where appropriate, can you invite a prospective client or partner to an event so they see your work in action?

Use Facebook or Instagram Live to stream an event or activity. Instead of hosting a private call where you answer questions, why not do it on a livestream so you can involve more people? If you are speaking at an event, can you livestream part of it or at least capture yourself backstage before you go on?

All of us work so hard to get big things done in our businesses. Let's make sure we take full advantage of this great work, by stacking as many opportunities as possible on each activity.

ACTION BREEDS INNOVATION

Two years into her business turnaround, Karley Cunningham of Big Bold Brand decided to apply for a grant for women entrepreneurs from the Canadian government. Seeing how well her Surefire Strategy was working for her clients, she was interested in codifying and digitizing the method so she could eventually license it to professionals and organizations who worked with entrepreneurs. Much to her delight, out of a pool of over 1,000 applicants, she got the $100,000 grant.

Karley spent a year codifying her method in detail and refining it in her client projects. This was so much work and was made extra difficult by a family tragedy when her younger sister

Leah got very sick and then died of cancer right in the middle of the project. Three times during the yearlong project, Karley texted me and said: "Tell me why I shouldn't just quit the project and give the money back." Knowing she was deep in stress and grief and in an extended eye of the needle moment, I didn't want to force her. "Your physical and emotional health is the most important thing," I said. "If you truly do not want to continue and it is too much, I completely support your decision. Why don't you allow yourself to rest and take a pause and let us extended team members take up some of the slack. Then you can decide how you want to proceed."

After each pause, and following reflection and discussion with her wife, Elise, she chose to keep going. Not because of some false sense of grind and hustle, but because she knew that her body of work had the ability to transform the businesses she worked with. She knew she would be contributing something that truly made a difference to the world of branding, and it would strengthen the work of her peers, partners, and customers in her ecosystem.

With support from an amazing working team, she completed the grant project. As soon as she was done, the world shut down during the Covid-19 pandemic.

Karley's Surefire Strategy method helped her clients not only navigate an upside-down world but come out thriving. Her business was no exception. Because she had codified and streamlined her operations, managing projects was easier and took less time. The seeds she had planted with her TMAs continued to bring new clients and she did not experience another downturn.

In May 2021, Big Bold Brand was selected as a Top 5 Finalist for Best Innovation for Small Business BC (British Columbia) out of over 900 submissions.

Karley will be the first to tell you that the journey from stalled entrepreneur to thriving, award-winning entrepreneur was not an easy path. She put in the work every day, one TMA at a time, to activate a flood of clients and build a substantial body of work. Because she was able to overcome a downturn on her entrepreneur journey, she will now be able to help thousands of her future clients and partners with a solid methodology and saleable product. What I witnessed as her coach was leadership growth forged by heart and fire.

Karley's business was transformed, and I was also changed by witnessing her courage. Because of her commitment to the process and many other courageous clients like her, I now know for sure that you don't have to trade your ethics to grow a great business. You can scale your business while helping other businesses grow around you.
And you can handle just about anything when you know that you are not alone on your business journey, and others will work hard to support your success.

EXERCISE: Ecosystem Marketing Review

To keep your business growing and your business culture healthy and dynamic, carve out time to complete this reflection on a quarterly or biannual basis.

Mission and Values

- Have we been consistent in our application of our principles, values, and ethics?
- Do we need to update our Always and Never lists?

Customers

- Do we still have the right customer segments?
- Do we need to adjust or refine our ideal customer problems?
- Are our offers designed to solve the problem we are best at solving?
- If not, who would be better?

Partnership Assessment

- Do we have the right partners?
- Are they delivering in a way consistent with our brand and values?
- What do we like best about this partnership?
- What do we want to fix in this partnership?
- Is there reciprocity at work?
- Is it profitable?

Staff Skills

- Do we have the right capabilities on our team?
- Are we over- or understaffed in any areas?
- Is there any step or process a person is doing that could be more efficiently done by automation?

Markets

- Who is here? Who is not here? Why aren't they here?

- Which new watering holes are we excited to explore next?

Marketing Analytics

- Are we meeting our KPIs?
- Are our metrics trending in the right direction?
- What do we need to fix to improve our numbers?

Product and Customer Experience

- What is bugging our customers?
- What is bugging us?
- What improvements can we make to remove obstacles that get in the way of solving our customer problems?

Leadership Behaviors

- What behaviors are getting in the way of building a vibrant company and ecosystem?
- What do we need to change in how we market and run our company to create a welcoming, equitable, and innovative environment for customers, employees, and partners from many different backgrounds?

CONCLUSION

I have had the blessing of 25 years as an entrepreneur. I appreciate all the clients and projects that have allowed me the freedom and flexibility to do the work I want to do, where, how, with whom, and when I want to do it. This work has provided for my family and extended family and for that I am extremely grateful.

By far, the most rewarding part of my business is the body of work my clients have brought to life in our work together. My clients have built programs that literally save lives. They have created tools and methods that have changed the way business is done. They have transformed the cultures of huge institutions, and the lives of audiences like business owners, leaders, doctors, lawyers, teachers, and families. They have built technology that makes life and work easier, more effective, and more efficient.

In not one engagement did I do this work alone. My vibrant ecosystem of peers, partners, collaborators, and mentors worked together to support the growth of my clients.

Now, my downtown Mesa neighbors, merchants, and partners are working together to create a city center that people far and wide will want to visit. We are building a place worth driving to on a Friday night from the suburbs because there is so much cool entertainment, great food, and fascinating shops. We are building a place where every person who walks down the street feels safe and respected and welcomed. We are building a place where we can gather in beautiful indoor and outdoor spaces to solve the deeper social issues in our city: improved education, affordable housing, economic and social equity, and climate change.

If you are tired of facing the fears and challenges of entrepreneurship alone, you don't have to. More and more of us each day are connecting, sharing, collaborating, and supporting each other's work in towns and cities across the world. We realize that working together, we are much more likely to generate abundance in an entire ecosystem, instead of small pockets of concentrated power and profit, while the vast majority of business owners struggle.

NOW IT'S UP TO YOU

Your customers, and their ecosystem partners, await your gifts, your talents, your tools, and your energy. They need the solution that only you can provide, in the unique way you choose to provide it. When you show your offers and share your thought leadership, they will utter words that will be music to your ears: "Where have you been? I have been waiting for a solution just like this."

If you work in corporate in a marketing or business development capacity, you face somewhat different challenges than entrepreneurs or small firms, but you still must identify and solve a customer problem, find new customers, develop compelling offers, and nurture long-term relationships. By applying concepts from this book, you will bring a breath of fresh of air to your organization.

The reality for businesses—whether large or small—is that they often don't grow for the same reason that we take the same route home from work every day, order the same meal at our favorite restaurant, and stick to comfortable routines in most areas of our lives. Most of us instinctively prefer the known to the unknown. In the absence of other factors, we unconsciously repeat ourselves, over and over again. Naturally, this causes us to repeat the same mistakes, too—in business and in life.

How does this manifest itself in marketing? Very often, after designing a product or service we think the market needs, we start looking for the customers or clients in all the old familiar places. Then we grow frustrated when hardly anyone shows up. Where is everybody? Well, they likely are in places we never thought to look.

The truth is the real world offers far more opportunity outside our field of vision than most businesspeople ever imagine. We need to remove our blinders of culture, background, and lived experience. We need to see beyond our comfortable social media cocoon and strive to understand the entirety of the marketplace, not just areas we already know.

But remember, while potential clients and customers can be found anywhere, they are not everywhere. Reaching out to the widest possible spectrum of potential customers is an inefficient and ineffective use of your resources. You need to find exactly where your customers hang out.

As I can attest, the Widest Net Method provides a proven method for identifying your best customers, discovering where they congregate, and connecting with them in a natural way that builds authentic and enduring relationships.

There is nothing theoretical or magical about the Widest Net Method. I developed it by working directly with individuals and entrepreneurial groups around the country. I've seen it generate new partnerships, expand markets and customers, and raise the thought leadership brand for countless clients. And if you're a bottom-line sort of person, I've witnessed the Widest Net Method generate millions of dollars of new revenue. Applied diligently, it works.

To recap:

Make sure the product or service you or your company is offering solves a problem worth solving and people are willing to pay to have their problem solved.

Accordingly, identify your ideal customers in terms of their problems, challenges, or aspirations. Add relevant demographic information to each audience profile. Finally, decide the people you want to work with and the people you don't want to work with.

Create an offer your ideal customer can't refuse, which means understanding the journey your ideal customers must undertake to solve their problem and providing an offer that helps them progress on their journey. Make sure every touchpoint your customer has with you and your organization is positive, congruent, and respectful of their values.

Nothing helps business owners grow more strategically and quickly than looking at their marketing through the lens of an ecosystem, which consists of all the services, products, organizations, events, and media that are aligned with your values and provide your ideal client with resources to solve their problem. Your ideal customer is at the center of that ecosystem.

Within this ecosystem are watering holes where your ideal customers reside, such as associations, events, podcasts, popular magazines, "best of" lists, and online groups. The organizers of these watering holes share a mission with you: to solve the core problem of your ideal client.

Reach out to members of your selected watering holes by sharing information and resources to support their work and solving your ideal customers' problems. Plant your seeds of connection slowly and methodically and break down your efforts into tiny marketing actions (TMAs).

Select a Beacon where you share your point of view and centralize your body of work for the benefit of your customers, partners, prospects, and anyone potentially interested in what you do. It could be a website, a podcast, a YouTube channel, or any other social media outlet.

Strive to create strong, mutually beneficial partnerships with other players in the ecosystem that already have established authentic relationships with your ideal customers. But don't rush into partnerships. Start slowly and build trust. Don't risk your reputation by partnering with an unvetted person or organization.

It's critical to become comfortable with the process of selling. Develop documents, resources, and answers to the most commonly asked questions from potential clients. Whatever sales method you use, make sure your sales approach is aligned with your values and congruent with your relationship building approach.

I'm confident that if you diligently apply the Widest Net Method and consistently implement TMAs, you will experience a regular flow of opportunities and requests for proposals. Where once you might have been stressed about not having enough clients, you may suddenly experience a new stress of having so many people approaching you that you have difficulty responding to everyone while servicing your existing clients.

This period, while exciting, can also be perilous because if you do not organize, operationalize, and get some help, you risk tanking the goodwill that has been developed by delivering excellent service to your clients. Anticipate this phase and develop a plan to build, strengthen, and streamline your operations. Remember you can't do everything alone.

DON'T BE A STRANGER

As this book rolls out and reaches new people and places, I can't wait to learn how you take the ideas and adapt and grow them in your business and community. I will share stories of your discoveries on my website at https://pamelaslim.com/thewidestnet.

Finally, I want you to know, unequivocally, that we all need each other.

Welcome home.

NOTES

CHAPTER 1

1. https://www.census.gov/newsroom/press-releases/2021
   /annual-business-survey.html.
2. https://genglobal.org/gew/about.

CHAPTER 3

1. https://fortune.com/fortune500/2020/search/.
2. https://www.statista.com/statistics/235494/new
   -entrepreneurial-businesses-in-the-us/.
3. https://www.amazon.com/4-Hour-Workweek-Expanded
   -Updated-Cutting-Edge-ebook/dp/B002WE46UW/ref=
   sr_1_2?crid=2UXI6I0ZAOFTX&dchild=1&keywords
   =ti.m+ferris+4+hour+work+week&qid=1617719020&spr
   efix=tim+ferris+4+hour+work%2Caps%2C167&sr=8-2.

CHAPTER 4

1. https://www.insidehighered.com/digital-learning
   /article/2019/01/16/study-offers-data-show-moocs-didnt
   -achieve-their-goals#.
2. https://www.intuit.com/company/corporate
   -responsibility/.
3. http://theleanstartup.com/principles.

4. https://quickbooks.intuit.com/oa/get-quickbooks/.

CHAPTER 5

1. Source: Crossbeam blog: https://blog.crossbeam.com /software-saas-era-ecosystems.
2. https://www.kauffman.org/ecosystem-playbook-draft-3/.
3. https://www.g2.com/products/crossbeam/reviews /crossbeam-review-4553221.
4. https://www.crossbeam.com/case-studies/zendesk/.

CHAPTER 7

1. https://www.understood.org/en/learning-thinking -differences/getting-started/what-you-need-to-know /learning-disabilities-by-the-numbers.
2. https://www.brookings.edu/innovation-districts/.

CHAPTER 8

1. https://www.amazon.com/gp/product/B008MCSHJ4/ref =dbs_a_def_rwt_hsch_vapi_tkin_p1_i1.

CHAPTER 9

1. https://firstround.com/review/the-founder-dating -playbook-heres-the-process-i-used-to-find-my-co -founder/.

CHAPTER 10

1. Marianna Mazzucato, *Mission Economy,* Harper Business, 2012.

INDEX

ABOUT THE AUTHOR

Pamela Slim is an author, community builder, business coach, and former director of Training and Development at Barclays Global Investors. She founded her company in 1996 and spent the first decade in business as a management consultant, creating and delivering training programs for large companies such as Charles Schwab, 3Com, Chevron and Cisco Systems.

Since 2005, Pam has advised thousands of entrepreneurs as well as companies serving the small business market such as Keap, GoDaddy, Progressive Insurance, and Prezi. Pam partnered with author Susan Cain to build and launch The Quiet Revolution.

Pam has written three books for entrepreneurs and creatives: *Escape from Cubicle Nation: From Corporate Prisoner to Thriving Entrepreneur* (Penguin/Portfolio 2009, named Best Small Business/Entrepreneur book of 2009 from Porchlight Books), *Body of Work: Finding the Thread That Ties Your Story Together* (Penguin/Portfolio 2014) and *The Widest Net: Unlock Untapped Markets and Discover New Customers Right in Front of You* (McGraw Hill, 2021).

In 2016, Pam and her husband Darryl cofounded the K'é Main Street Learning Lab in Mesa, Arizona, a grassroots, community-led learning lab for BIPOC entrepreneurial leaders.